THE ENGLISH INN
PAST AND PRESENT

MARKET DAY OUTSIDE THE OLD RED LION AT GREENWICH

From an original drawing by Rowlandson, hitherto unpublished.

THE ENGLISH INN
PAST AND PRESENT

A REVIEW OF ITS HISTORY
AND SOCIAL LIFE

BY

A. E. RICHARDSON, F.S.A.,

Author of " Monumental Classic Architecture "

H. DONALDSON EBERLEIN, B.A.,

Author of " The Practical Book of Period Decoration "

BENJAMIN BLOM  New York/London 1968

First Published 1925
Reissued 1968 by
Benjamin Blom, Inc., Bronx, New York 10452
and 56 Doughty Street, London, W.C. 1
Library of Congress Catalog Card Number 68-56499

Printed in U.S.A. by
NOBLE OFFSET PRINTERS, INC.
NEW YORK 3, N. Y.

TO

SAMUEL HOWARD WHITBREAD, Esquire,
C.B., M.A., J.P.

Lord Lieutenant for the County of
Bedfordshire

This work is by his permission dedicated
as an acknowledgment of his interest in
English traditional life.

ERRATUM.

Page 247, Fig. 245: *For* "Scarf" *read* "Scharf"

PREFACE

The inn has played a large part in the domestic life of England down the centuries. Always intimately associated with the characteristics of the English people as a centre for social life, it still retains a warm place in their hearts. The story of the tavern therefore is associated with the tale of the road and English wayfaring life. Love of travel is a strong characteristic of the English race, yet it co-exists with a feeling for home comforts and a desire to be reminded of familiar things. Thus it is, from the earliest times, that the inn, in spite of its widened functions, has at each stage of its development retained the piquant element of domesticity. The old inns of England are unlike those of other countries. The majority are genuine survivals ; they are records of other times and customs and they have a symbolic value to the ordinary traveller. They are generally simple in character, but many have undergone alterations and changes corresponding with each era of social progress. The inns of each period, especially such as remain intact and unaltered, could be described in any treatise dealing with the recognised phases of house building ; collectively they present a subject for a monograph.

A number of excellent books have been issued dealing with inns and coaching from the anecdotal and descriptive point of view, and the literature on the subject is an extensive and growing one, but it seemed to us that there was room for a fairly comprehensive survey of the inn, considered both as a structure and as a repository of social life.

As buildings the inns are of the highest appeal, both for their own account and for the centuries of human intercourse, which, to some extent, may be considered as enshrined in them ; we have attempted to range over the subject from the point of view of its historical development, starting with a brief glance at the mediæval inn and continuing through Tudor and Stuart times to the eighteenth century, with matter relevant to the coaching era, and from thence carrying on the story, through the temporary eclipse brought about by the rise of the railways, to the present day.

The inns described and illustrated in this book will be found to include most of the chief examples in England, representing each development of the national building tradition, from the fourteenth to the early nineteenth centuries. While admitting that certain inns and taverns have not been included, it should be understood that a complete account of every inn of moment would mean a book of greater scope. The work of gathering the material has entailed journeys on all the main and chief cross-roads of England. By such travels the writers have discovered certain inns off the regular track, and were brought into touch with facts and details of unrecorded history. With the revival of road travel, the inn has taken on a newer significance. Proprietors are now applying to architects for advice when remodelling or repairing their premises, and there is also a marked difference in the style of the new inns and taverns which are being built under expert advice. People touring the country are beginning to select their inn with an eye to its pictorial amenity. Coinciding with this revived interest it is to be hoped that this work will do something to bring about a yet increased appreciation of the subject as a whole and provide a record for reference of the buildings described.

Our warm and grateful acknowledgments must be given to Mr. Roger Ramsdell, of New York, who has co-operated effectively in a number of ways, and we also desire to thank our publishers for placing at our disposal their invaluable collection of material.

A. E. R.
H. D. E.

October, 1925.

NOTE OF ACKNOWLEDGMENT

As in the case of the " Smaller English House," we have to thank Mr. Oswald Doughty, M.A., B.Litt., of University College, London, for kindly overhauling the text and making many valuable suggestions. Mr. Ambrose Heal has permitted the reproduction, from his fine collection, of a number of old trade cards and bills. The frontispiece, in colour, is a reproduction from a drawing in the Royal Naval College, Greenwich, by kind permission of the Lords Commissioners of the Admiralty. For a number of subjects from MSS and old drawings, we have to thank the authorities of the British Museum, the Bodleian Library, Oxford, and the Fitzwilliam Museum, Cambridge, while Figs. 38 and 48 are from the Victoria and Albert Museum, South Kensington. Several London subjects are from the lately dispersed Gardner collection. We have to thank Mr. Walford, of New Oxford Street, for many kindnesses in allowing us to refer to and make use of his extensive topographical collection. We are exceedingly grateful to Messrs. Ellis and Smith, of Grafton Street, London, for kindly giving us access to their fine collection of old prints and drawings, from which several subjects have been included. The view of Dartford High Street was formerly in the collection of Mr. Basil Dighton, of Savile Row, and is reproduced with his consent. Our thanks are also due to Mr. Hector Corfiato, S A.D.G., for the series of road maps, which he specially prepared for the final chapter of this volume.

Mr. Hugh Mottram, A.R.I.B.A., has very kindly allowed us to include several subjects from his interesting series of drawings of old inns. Mr. Hanslip Fletcher has allowed the inclusion of two charming drawings which are reproduced in Figs. 108 and 237. Mr. F. J. Watson Hart has permitted us to include his drawing of the Mermaid at Rye (Fig. 59), and Mr. Roland W. Paul, F.S.A., has sanctioned the reproduction of his drawing of the Bell Inn, Holborn. Figs. 191, 192, 204 and page 252 are drawn by Mr. Basil Oliver, F.R.I.B.A., and reproduced from his " Old Cottages in East Anglia." Fig. 205, the Sign of the Bell,

Bruton, is from a drawing by Mr. E. Guy Dawber, P.R.I.B.A., Fig. 273 is from a drawing by Mr. W. H. Bidlake, F.R.I.B.A., and Fig. 202 by W. Curtis Green, A.R.A., from "Old Surrey Cottages," and Figs. 188, 203, 225, 270, by Sidney R. Jones.

With regard to photographs, Mr. Herbert Felton, F.R.P.S., has taken a number of photographs specially ; others are included from a series originally taken by him. To Messrs. F. Frith and Co., Reigate, we owe Figs. 27, 65, 72, 79, 103, 115, 173, 233, 234, 235, 250, 264, 267 ; Messrs. Valentine and Sons, Limited, of Dundee, Figs. 55, 82, 104, 241, 274 ; other subjects are from the Publishers' collection, taken by the late Mr. W. Galsworthy Davie and Mr. Horace Dan. Other attributions are as follows : a number have been specially commissioned. Mr. Allbone, St. Neots, Figs. 52, 99 ; Messrs. Dolby, of Stamford, Fig. 116 ; The Doncaster Rotophoto Co., Fig. 102 ; Mr. George Hepworth, Brighouse, Yorks, Figs. 275, 276 ; Mr. Bernard Griffin, Dorchester, Figs. 118, 119, 178, 206, 266 ; Mr. W. Harper, Ludlow, Figs. 92 and 93 ; Mr. H. Jarman, Bury St. Edmunds, Fig. 43 ; Mr. C. King, Lymington, Fig. 180 ; Messrs. T. B. Latchmore and Sons, Hitchin, Fig. 244 ; Mr. H. Manistre, Thame, Fig. 44 ; Mr. G. Moss, Christchurch, Figs. 114, 123, 214 ; Mr. H. Pickwell, Streatham, Figs. 76 and 77 ; Mr. E. C. Pulbrook, Fig. 243 ; Messrs. W. H. Smith and Sons (Kingsway series), Fig. 1 (lower) and Fig. 75 ; Mr. C. A. Stockbridge, Culford, Bury St. Edmunds, Fig. 236 ; Mr. W. Tams, Cambridge, Fig. 32 ; Messrs. H. W. Taunt, Oxford, Figs. 67, 101, 127, 246, 254, 255, 258 ; Messrs. Tompkins and Barrett, Swindon, Fig. 210 ; Mr. Whiffen, Poplar, Figs. 133, 138, 142 ; Mr. F. C. Williams, Towcester, Fig. 86.

CONTENTS

xi

Small Inn at Bishop's Stortford.

The Three Fishes, Turvey, Bedfordshire.

FIG. 1. TWO OLD INNS OF RURAL ENGLAND.

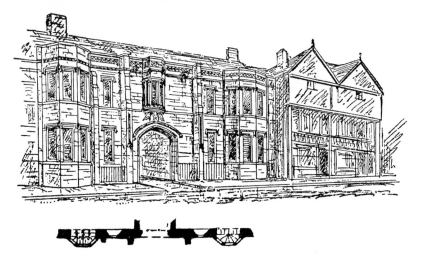

THE ANGEL INN, GRANTHAM.

CHAPTER I

INTRODUCTION

We are all fond of visualising old scenes, and attempting a reconstruction of the life and manners of other days. It is, therefore, comforting to find that progress, which in some of its workings has acted to the detriment of things companionable, has at least recognised the merit of inns. To the English the inn is a place of entertainment, a kind of institution which from the earliest times has served as the mirror up to Nature, and from whence, in alliance with the Church, come the first ideas of stagecraft. Of all countries England is richest in associations of this kind, for the best of old inns stand much as our ancestors knew them. We find such houses on lonely heaths, or fronting village greens, recording the peculiarities of ancient or local custom. We are delighted with the accumulated variety of taverns and hostelries in the streets of country towns, and the larger type in the cathedral cities, in all the seclusion of side streets and alleys. There is the modest inn by the side of a river, with its entourage of pleasure gardens and shady arbours ; quite distinct is the equally pleasant seaside tavern with its circular windows wide to the horizon. The alehouses, which are the poor relations in the hierarchy of inns, have their place in remote hamlets. As we wander in the paths of antiquity, from town to town, and from one county to another, it is brought to our eyes that no two inns are alike. We begin to emancipate our thoughts from the common-place, to understand the distinctions arising from unequal causes recording the traditions of centuries. The symbol of welcome is scarred deep in the fashioning of inns ; they are related to domestic architecture, but their character is different.

It has been our good fortune to have our roving passion satisfied. We have made a point of studying almost every tavern that showed pictorial as well as historical merit. There is something in the appeal of the common hearth, and the liberty of a sheltering roof, outweighing the distinctions of ordinary society. Few there are who do not respect the rambling oddities, the faded magnificence, the low or lofty rooms, the heavy furniture, and the multitudinous details. Our earnest desire to know, to see, and to handle, has led in turn to an appraising of antique plate, to a search for prints and engravings, and a subsequent endeavour to piece the data into a story. We have wandered, sketch-books in hand, to make our inventory. As we look over the memoranda and recall our impressions, there is one thought that constantly recurs—the very material as well as the structural entity of an inn is vibrant with mellowed associations. Kings and beggars have entered or turned from the doors ; strange faces have peered from the windows. It becomes clear on reflection that an inn has its own ethics of freemasonry. By law and courtesy all are free to claim hospitality ; but the true possessors are the ghostly participants of every feast, who may be said to haunt every nook, and who hold their right by mortmain.

The innholder has especial advantages : there is the opportunity to look after others, the perpetual curatorship, the building up or the maintenance of the reputation of the house. The guest enjoys the excitement of inn life, the novelty of strange beds and unaccustomed surroundings—all so familiar and yet so different from home.

No idle humour takes us to inns. The joy is not so much in the actual stay as in the half-remembered vision. We carry with us thoughts of walls and furnishings, the music of knives and forks, the faint or aggressive flavour of cooking, and the blurred shapes of the chairs and tables. The secrets, the mystery and the charm inhere in the memory. No account of the English inn could, or should, be allowed to begin from any other centre but London, for although the hostelries of real antiquity are few, the streets within the old boundaries have preserved deformities which are sympathetic with the past. Thus it becomes an art to extract incidents from everyday life in London which bear on the subject. The very complexion of the moving crowd, the closely packed traffic, the noise and the uproar, occasions a welling up in the throat and tears for the pageant that was and is. Beginning with all we have heard or read of old London inns, we will attempt the first reconstruction. It is best done in the evening, when the City is deserted, for then can be visualised localities which from the earliest times were the halting places for travellers. From the gallery above the Dome of St. Paul's we look down on the streets and alleys which recall the mediæval formation. There are the distant heights above the bricky growth, familiar landmarks that seemed to check the close packed streets. What other city arouses such interest and curiosity ? Wren's churches and steeples mark the positions of buildings destroyed in the Great Fire, and, although the ancient hostelries and inn yards have disappeared, the spell of antiquity hovers above the City, an ever vital charm. Thus it is to London we turn as the true inn centre, for the mother of cities has reserved to herself the secret of preserving landmarks. All Londoners have at heart the mystery of their city ; they may not all be able to enter into the spirit of the past, but there are the facts of the narrow streets, of the old buildings, the prints, maps and engravings, the written word of the venerable Stow, and a host of guidebooks from Hatton to Weale to inspire confidence. We have said that old London is to be seen at its best on a summer's evening, when the lifeblood has temporarily left the arteries. It was on such an evening that thoughts of a mediæval tavern, *The Mermaid*, in Cornhill, were conjured up and an attempt made to depict a scene of other days.

THE FIFTEENTH CENTURY INN.

We will imagine a walk from old St. Paul's to Cornhill along Chepe on an October afternoon in 1420. The steeple of the cathedral towers above the houses, the hundred churches, the monasteries and the Guildhall. Cheapside appears of abnormal width, with fountains and conduits along the centre. Beyond London Bridge is the grey mass of the Tower. There are many people in the streets, for curfew will not sound from Saint Martin's for two hours. Since early morning the din of the city has followed travellers on the roads beyond the walls and spent itself over the fields as far as the neighbouring hills. Packhorses (Fig. 33) and carts have clattered through the streets, the hucksters have been busy at their stalls, while the goldsmiths, armourers, and

merchants, have maintained activity.   Some of the rabble are returning
from an execution on Tower Hill.   There are carts in the streets, broad-
tyred, some drawn by a single horse, as well as barrows pulled by huge
dogs, three in a line, directed by their master, who gives warning of
approach by a blast on a horn.   The iron tyres have crushed the paving
of cobbles and flints a foot deep in mire.   The apprentices are still
bawling from the open shops, armed men are marching to relieve guard
at the gates, and there are the shambling figures of friars and Capuchins
moving like automata to a clangour of bells from the churches and
monasteries.   The day has been active for trade and free from riot,
the masons have been at work, the women cheapening food and wearing
apparel, and scores of country folk are in town from the adjoining
villages.   London at this time is as prosperous as any city of the Netherlands, the people love the noise, respect the Lord Mayor and Aldermen,
reverence the nobles, envy the goldsmiths and tolerate the foreigner
within their gates.   With the hour of five work will gradually cease,
for all anticipate a bout of drinking at the taverns.   We continue our
walk along Chepe, glancing at the massive timbers of the houses, some
with projecting storeys, and others rising flat-fronted on a plinth of
stone.   The roofs are of steep pitch, somewhat fantastic, with gables
to the street.   Most of the roofs are covered with thatch freshly limed
as a precaution against fire.   The windows are without glass, but all
have wooden shutters.   At the window openings are the women, some
sewing, others gossiping, and all taking an interest in the people below.
Here an apprentice is placing a lanthorn in its wrought iron bracket
against the time when the watch will inspect the lighting of the ward.
In our mood of retrospection we observe the small taverns at the heads
of the alleys, and note the signs of *The Bush, The Grapes,* or *The Angel,*
and in our thoughts catch a babel of sound, including oaths and ribald
ballads.   Externally the small inns appear to have the same character
as the houses.   For the time being modern London has vanished; in
its place we see an earlier city, and so we proceed through the width
of Chepe to Cornhill.   This large house with the painted sign and the
low entry must be *The Mermaid.*   The oaken door has heavy strap
hinges and a ring of iron.   The drawer is in attendance.   We pass in to
the first entry, which is low and heavily beamed, and notice a narrow
table at the centre, around which, seated on stools, are soldiers off duty
from the Tower.

Beyond the first entry is the chief room of the tavern, having noble
proportions and an open-timbered roof.   There is a screen at the further

end with a gallery over, richly traceried and carved. The log fire on the stone hearth throws light and shade on the grotesques supporting the upper part of the chimney, and escaping wisps of smoke circle upwards to the roof timbers. There is little furniture ; what is there is of oak. The most important table is the one near the fire, and the company at this table first attracts our attention. Our thoughts carry us still further. There are the portly figures of two city merchants, capped and cloaked, in close talk with two sharp-visaged sea-captains of London Town, due to take their ships out of the Thames on the next tide, and here for final instructions. There is a squire lately arrived from Saffron Walden, whose interest is wool stapling, a lawyer attending the squire, a city alderman and his friend, a grocer. A party of armourers occupy a table at a respectful distance from the first group. The floor is covered with rushes that have been trodden for the past month, affording safe harbourage to the healthy black rats who seem scornful of the dogs snuffling for bones. No one seems to mind the smell of stale food, of animals and humans. On each table there are blackjacks filled with strong ale. The merchants are speeding their venture with hot spiced ale, the lawyer and the squire drink Rhenish wine from silver mazers, while the captains await their fourth bottle of Bordeaux and look discontentedly at their empty glasses. There are cries of " Drawer, Drawer ! " without, answered by " Anon, Anon ! " from behind the screen. Then the serving men appear, with their leathern aprons and tight-fitting round caps, from the top of the stone steps leading to the vaulted cellars where, under the eye of the cellarer, they have been filling the drinking vessels and keeping score with tally sticks. The conversation becomes general. The lawyer speaks of the ordinance restricting the projection of ale stakes in Chepe, the alderman replies regarding the fine to be imposed on offenders, and the landlord makes up his mind to effect an alteration to the sign of *The Mermaid* above his door. And so we picture the scene as the light fails and the shadows deepen, until at the first sound of curfew the drawers and the cellar-men, led by the host, collect the score and show the company to the door, for *The Mermaid* is a house of repute. But the case is different with the smaller taverns where are foregathered the drovers, carters, waggoners and porters, with a contingent of loafers, cutpurses, mummers and thieves.

The scene fades ; we are on the steps of the Royal Exchange in the midst of modern London, with the Bank of England being brought to the dust, and the gaunt shape of the Mansion House confronting us.

In this sketch we have attempted a view of the better class tavern of Plantagenet times such as existed in many English cities. We call to mind that the nobles had their palaces within the walls and near the banks of the river, that the merchants had fair houses and gardens, while the craftsmen lived with their families, often two or three households under one roof.

As far as can be understood the city tavern was distinct from the inn, which latter provided sleeping accommodation as well as stabling and stores for goods. The hostelries proper were in close proximity to the gates which gave on to the main highways. To such inns came the carriers from Essex, Suffolk and Norfolk, from the Midland shires, from Oxford, Gloucester and the West Country. The inns of Southwark were frequented by the men of Kent, Surrey and Sussex.

It will be gathered from a study of old documents, as well as from such examples that exist, that the inn of Plantagenet times was rectangular in plan, the apartments being grouped four-square about a court with external galleries to each floor (Fig. 61). A heavy oak gate shut the court at night. Beyond the main courtyard ran a lesser court, about which the stables were grouped, and this had its own gate to a lane in the rear.

Life in London in these times was strenuous. In winter men huddled round the fire for light and warmth. They rose and dressed in the dark, and the cobbled street clattered early to the packhorse trains making for the Middlesex forest or the treacherous roads of Epping, Waltham and Hainhault. Travellers there were in plenty, but they rode in company, for the laws, stringent as they were, did not deter the robbers. Outside London and other towns the inns of the Middle Ages, as well as the monastic houses, accommodated travellers. They were the counterparts of the London inn, the tavern and the alehouse.

The Mermaid at Cornhill has been selected as a starting point for this narrative, because it represented the typical London house of its day, as well as for the fact that London was the bourne of all " travaillers." The inn of the fifteenth century is perhaps the safest to discuss, by reason of the examples that exist. It might have been more accurate to have begun with an account of the Tabard, but who would dare to restate Chaucer ? Another phase of the subject could have been entered upon in a description of the guest houses for pilgrims, such as those that existed at Canterbury, Glastonbury, Bedford, Gloucester and St. Albans ; such appendages to monastic establishments were intended for the benefit of the better classes, and were far superior to the timbered barns which served as dormitories for the peasants. We are, however, concerned with the connection of the subject to trade, religion and political events. In the fifteenth century the chief inns were largely built of stone; they differed but little in style from the monastic buildings, the castles and churches. Thus we find, from the examples of this period which are still extant, very slight changes in outward aspect other than those necessitated by the employment of local material and the details of windows, doors and decoration. Our quest for the fifteenth century inn took us from London to Grantham, along the road from Shoreditch Church to Huntingdon, with a detour to *The Lion* at Buckden, a house built in 1477. This was the highway for those who journeyed between London and York in charge of pack trains. As the journey was made, the meaning of the inn signs was discussed; the number of Georges, Lions and Horses—white and black —brought to mind the intimacies of mediæval social life. There is no sign of *The Talbot* on the North Road, yet the name was familiar to the packmen as denoting the breed of dogs trained to guard their goods.

With our minds centred on the aspect of the fifteenth century, we looked upon the stone front of *The Angel* at Grantham (Figs. 1, 13 and 14) with feelings of respectful enquiry. It stands in the middle of the town, facing the Market Square and the ancient cross, a guardian of the North Road from the late fourteenth century, a silent witness to the momentous events of peace and war. Gone are its more ancient glories, the galleries and external stairways, the timber-built wing to the right of the front, and the rambling barns at the back. There have been many later additions (Fig. 105), interesting as relics of travel and having a place in the sequence of the life of the house, but at this stage we are concerned with its aspect on the night of the 19th of October, 1483, when Richard the Third was housed within.

Seated in the oriel window of the room on the ground floor to the left of the entry we speculated on the former character of the house, and endeavoured to reconstruct the development that had taken place in social life between the years 1420-1483. It was assumed that few changes had occurred in the matter or manner of building during these sixty-three years. The monasteries were intact, so were the pilgrim inns and "Royal houses" in various parts of the country. In London at this time rumours were toward of the movement against Richard, and the Duke of Buckingham had the sympathy of the people ; but it is in the long room forming the first floor of the "Maison du

Roi " that a significant incident in history was enacted. We thought
of a pack train approaching the town, making for York, the merchants
discussing political events ; the packmen, and the dogs, already six days
on the road, sore tired, the gloom of the North Road having affected
both man and beast. Perhaps it is a matter of urgency that the train
enters Grantham before dusk and inns at *The Woolpack*, for *The Angel*
this day is closed to ordinary men. As these ruminations were
continued, we thought of the King signing the death warrant of the
Duke of Buckingham in the room above. We had a picture of the town
in the gathering dusk of the October evening with the twinkling of
torches, the assembly of men-at-arms, archers and crossbowmen, of
soldiers billeted in the houses of the townspeople, of the King's archers
standing at the entry of *The Angel* the open oak doors of which reveal
horses and messengers. How little has changed, and yet how much !
The torchlight of 1483 lit up the embayed façade and flicked the tracery
before us ; it showed up the deep recessing and the regal integrity of the
building. In the fifteenth century, suspended from a heavy oak frame,
there was a painted sign of an angel with a flaming sword. From the
adjoining buttress projected a stave, at the end of which was carved
the sign of a bush. We pictured the house as it appeared to the entourage
of the King lodged in the neighbouring buildings. We thought of the
knights and officers who used this room, of the rush-strewn floor, the log
fire, the ceiling beams, the grotesque heads, and the tapestried walls.
The apartment in which the King lodged then extended the whole length
of the first floor.   There are still to be seen the two stone mullioned
bay windows, following the lines of those below, one at each end of
the room. At the centre is the semi-circular oriel with a raised seat,
from whence can be viewed the Cross in the Market Square. We pictured
Richard the Third and his attendants, the halberdiers on guard and the
firelight showing up the tapestried scenes of Biblical subjects.

It would be impertinent to attempt to dramatise the scene or to
give personality to the characters. They must remain hazy and indis-
tinct, but we can imagine the scene, the marshalling of the troops, the
stopping of the pack trains till the King and his following have departed,
the splendour of the cavalcade, and the pageantry of the mediæval
setting. It is above such things that the gilded angel has cast its sightless
eyes, as well as over the stone heads of King Edward and Queen
Philippa. There are many other inns which claim to be of the fifteenth
century, and perhaps the claim is true when some part of their fabric
is considered, such as the timbered framing of the ceilings within *The*

Lion at Buckden, the vaulted cellars of *The Mitre* at Oxford, or those
of the crypt of *The George* at Rochester.   At Bedford, on the west side
of the High Street, is a venerable relic, *The George,* a stone-built house
standing practically as it did when Buckler drew it in 1837 (Fig. 19).
There is *The Falstaff* at Canterbury (Fig. 92), *The Fighting Cocks* at
St. Albans (Fig. 63), *The George* at Glastonbury, built in 1475 (Fig. 60)
The George at Norton St. Philip (Fig. 66 and p. 59), and other houses
of mediæval character which have an affinity with *The Angel* at
Grantham.   At Compton is a house which was once a pilgrims' hostel.
There is the timber structure of *The Star* at Alfriston (Fig. 65) and that
delightful specimen of old Sussex architecture, *The Pilgrims' Hostel* at
Battle, as well as *The New Inn* at Gloucester (Fig. 61), the latter strangely
altered from the form which tradition asserts was given to it by the
monk John Twynning.   Visitors to St. Albans would scarcely expect
to find a pilgrims' hostel of the fifteenth century within the scarlet
brick front of *The George,* but this house is indubitably a survivor
from the times when the Monastery guarded the relics of St. Alban.
And so we could go on speculating on the origin of pilgrim hostels and
monastic inns, such as *The George* at Winchcombe, *The Lord Crewe
Arms* at Blanchland, and that fine mediæval relic *The King's Head*
at Aylesbury (Fig. 72).   It is to be regretted that so few of the real
mediæval inns remain for our delight and curiosity.   Gone are the
old inns of Southwark, swept into the limbo of the past in the fires of
the seventeenth century, while London has suffered her ancient houses,
even those that escaped the Fire, to be brought to the dust.   From the
topography of London, however, as well as from the mediæval inns
of the country towns, some idea can be conjured up of this early, if not
earliest, phase of inn life and custom.

The Sixteenth Century Inn.

Unlike any other aspect of English domestic architecture, the inn
as a subject for technical description does not present itself in complete
purity of style.   At best it represents development and change ;
additions have been made at all periods without regard to the original
theme ; hence it is easier to describe the inn as it is rather than as it
once stood.   In this general introductory we have found it expedient
to return continually to London for matter relative to the inn of different
periods.   The transition from the fifteenth to the sixteenth century
was not a time for the development of the national architecture, although

it must be conceded that, despite the suppression of the monasteries
and the ensuing years of religious dissension, the domestic qualities of
Tudor architecture were extended from the traditions of the fifteenth
century until they, too, became merged with the newer leavening of
renaissance detail. Few inns were built at this time, but the old hostels
were altered and adapted, for the suppression of the monastic houses
gave freer scope to private enterprise ; but travellers were content to
make use of derelict buildings for the purpose of accommodation. At

FIG. 2.—INTERIOR OF AN EARLY SIXTEENTH CENTURY TAVERN

this juncture the inn became more closely associated with trading
between towns ; it had, at this date, 1590, lost its religious significance
as a halting place for pilgrims and now took on the true import of a rest
house for men of business.

In our thoughts we must investigate the Cheapside of the sixteenth
century, with its ancient houses, conduits, shops, stalls and projecting
signs. At this date some of the timbered houses have been rebuilt.
It is obviously a new world, quite different from that of the fifteenth

century. In London, Sir Thomas Gresham is chief amongst the merchants; he has lately superintended the building of the Royal Exchange; trade is firmly established, and Europe takes its lead in commerce from London. We have selected the year 1590, in the month of September, as the date of our enquiry into the events of the day. Two years have passed since the defeat of the Armada; Queen Elizabeth is at the zenith of her power, the age is one of enterprise and adventure. Men are wondering at the power of the printing press, scholars are translating the classics, poets and actors adapting old themes. From uncharted seas captains are bringing back strange stories. The memory of the deliverance from Spain, of the persecution of the Huguenots and of the days of burning at the stake are too fresh to be disregarded, even at this merry hour.

Cheapside and Cornhill can now boast some new taverns as well as those of earlier origin. We think of them frequented by the bronzed and bearded adventurers—the John Oxenhams and followers of Drake and Raleigh; eager-faced, lean, lank and scurvy marked, with piercing deep-set eyes, men who have seen the Guinea Coast, the Cape and the Indian Seas, adventurous spirits to whom the lonely wastes of the Atlantic are familiar from Plymouth Cattewater to the shores of Virginia. Now within the London taverns they drink, smoke, and plot new ventures.

As we reconstruct the scene so the picture becomes clear in its details. It is an autumn morning; there are crowds in Chepe and near the Exchange. There are gallants attired in the expensive French fashion, ruffed and scented, with neatly trimmed beards short and peaked; perhaps they are about to dine at *The Three Tuns*, Newgate, *The Boar's Head* by London Stone, or the ancient *Mermaid* in Cornhill.

The Cheapside tavern, as we fancy it, is a gabled house of four storeys, having canted bay windows and richly-carved panels. There is a door at the centre, and the lintel over the door is carved with orna-ment resembling a grape vine. We envision a long room with two tables and many stools. There are many guests, whose wants are attended by youthful waiters. Wooden platters, knives and wooden salt-cellars are in use. The fare is pork and souse, followed by a roast capon, and ended with a pudding which is served on the reverse of the wooden platters. Some have finished the victuals and are enjoying mazers of sack, with clean pipes and Virginian tobacco as finishing luxuries.

So much for the Elizabethan eating-house, the famous taverns which Shakespeare knew and Ben Jonson and his circle frequented.

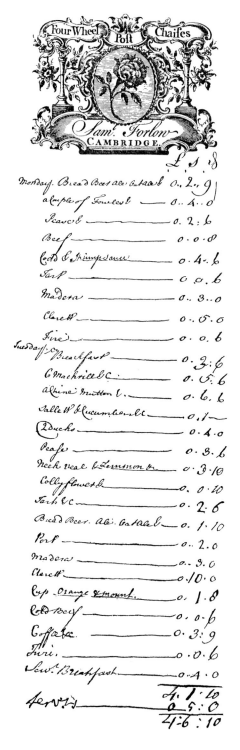

FIG. 3.—CONTRASTS IN BILLS:
THE ROSE, CAMBRIDGE.

It is a pleasant pastime conjuring up the atmosphere of the London tavern of that day.

From the tavern we turn to the Elizabethan inn, of which, in the late sixteenth century, many had been newly built, both in London and in the country towns and villages. The newer type of inn had arisen in response to the needs of the day; it had been occasioned to some extent by the revival of trade. There were, however, the older establishments, many of them dating from the late fifteenth century, as well as those of a still earlier origin; such were renowned throughout the land and known to all travellers.

At this period *The Tabard* in Southwark was the chief centre for travellers and goods from Kent, Surrey and Sussex. At *The Bull and Mouth*, near St. Martin's le Grand, and the inns of Aldersgate, were to be seen people and carriers from the Midlands and the north. Hard by Bishopsgate and Aldgate were the newer inns, augmenting the older houses where from the earliest times travellers from East Anglia had inned. The function of the inn had increased; it was now a

Fig. 6. TRADE CARD OF THE TURK'S-HEAD, NEWCASTLE. (About 1830.)

Figs. 4 and 5. BILLS OF THE BELL, STILTON.

14

Fig. 9.   A BUSY TIME IN A CELLAR, AND A   COURTYARD WELL.
(XIIIth Century MS.)

FIG. 12. A XVITH CENTURY JOY-RIDE IN SPRING.

FIG. 10 A XVTH CENTURY CELLARER.

FIG. 11.
NINEPINS BEFORE THE INN, EARLY XVITH CENTURY.
(Contemporary MS.)

FIG. 13.   The Front.   (XVth Century.)

FIG. 14.   Vaulting of one of the bay windows.

THE ANGEL, GRANTHAM.   (*v. also page* 1.)

business centre to which goods could be despatched to await delivery. As in Plantagenet and early Tudor times, the packhorse train formed the most convenient way of transferring goods from town to town, although there were waggons of a cumbrous type—some two and others four-wheeled—drawn by horses or oxen. For elderly people there was the horse-borne litter or palanquin; courtiers and gentlemen rode their own horses, attended in princely state by many servants. The landlords welcomed all such travellers. The buildings, while retaining certain characteristics of the inns of previous periods, had innovations, such as special rooms for the rich and privileged.

The Bull and Mouth has long vanished, like the mythical bull which the Cretonian " ate up whole." The site has long been lost beneath the foundations of the Post Office, not inappropriately built on the ruins of a house which for centuries served as a means of communication between London and the country, but this official building in its turn has been pulled down and its foundations swept away.

Direct evidence of the aspect of *The Bull and Mouth* as it appeared in the late sixteenth century is not forthcoming, but we try to think of it as it might have appeared on a September morning in 1590.

At the first sign of dawn there are sounds of movement within the house and about the yard, for a pack train, some thirty strong in horses, a dozen men and six talbot dogs, is due to start for Coventry. The men in charge and the hostlers are attending to the loading of the pack-saddles, while the chief packman is in the " ostry " settling the score with the landlord. Momentary excitement follows the arrival of two horsemen, members of Lord Burleigh's secret police, who have ridden through the night. In the rooms around the gallery some guests are arising, doors are opened and heads pop out to sample the morning. From the neighbouring yards can be heard the crowing of cocks and the barking of dogs, the first of the sounds that Elizabethan London is hearing on entering on another day. No such noise disturbs the guests in the best chamber called the Solar. This is an oak-panelled room with a richly patterned plaster ceiling and an ornate chimneypiece; the furniture is in the somewhat heavy taste of the time. Sheltered within the Utrecht velvet-curtained bed is a squire from Huntingdon, up in town to do business with his lawyer in the Middle Temple. His daughter and her tiring woman sleep in the adjoining room. There are other apartments, less expensive, holding learned doctors from the University of Cambridge, divines from Ely and Norwich, and not a few country gentlemen.

For further and first hand accounts of the Elizabethan inn the reader must examine *The Reindeer* at Banbury, the gates of which have the date 1570, and the remains of the famous " Globe Room " built in 1637 (Fig. 78).　Such examples as *The Dolphin* at Heigham, near Norwich (Fig. 64), parts of which date from 1587, *The Hog's Head* or *The Greyhound* at Thame, *The Crown and Treaty* at Uxbridge and *The Three Crowns* at Chagford, *The Ostrich* at Colnbrook (Figs. 70, 73), *The Swan* at Elstow (Fig. 238), and the famous example at Scole (Figs. 80, 81, 95), show types of the sixteenth and seventeenth century inn at its best.　When Mr. Edwards started his tour of the eastern counties some fifty odd years since, he recorded a chain of Elizabethan inns from Aldgate Pump to Norwich, some of which still exist, but the larger house of the period is becoming rarer.

From the death of Queen Elizabeth to the opening years of the Civil Wars the Elizabethan inn continued to flourish in spite of the decline of certain industries and crafts.　Under Cromwell little encouragement was given to trade, thus accounting for the fact that few roads were improved or new inns built.　London, however, at the time of the Restoration appeared much as it was at the close of the sixteenth century ; many old buildings had been altered, patched and newly covered with plaster.　The tenements in the alleys were crowded with several families, the inns had survived the Puritan ban and now echoed to ballads in honour of the King.　This period is now considered to have formed a curious transitionary stage from things mediæval ; it was, in other words, an age of compromise as well as one countenancing the retention of certain old customs.

There are at least three seventeenth century inns which have a right to be considered as representative of the period.　The earliest is *The Lygon Arms*, at Broadway (Figs. 85, 95), a house rich in picturesque detail and appointments ; the second is *The Haycock* (Figs. 20-22), at Wansford, near Stamford, on the Great North Road, which ranks as the largest stone-built inn of the century and one which reveals the Cotswold tradition extending as far North as the River Nene.　The Haycock is said to have taken its name from the legend of a man who fell asleep on a haycock, and the river rising, carried him and his strange craft from near Peterborough to the buttress of the stone bridge at Wansford.　The sudden jar against the bridge awakened the rustic, who enquired of a farmer where he was.　" At Wansford," was the reply.　" In England ? " queried the man.　And from that time, Wansford has always been described as " in England."　Whatever the truth of the tale, the Haycock was taken as the sign for the adjoining inn, and so it remained until some years since, when the house went into retirement as a place of call.   The third inn is the rambling, now almost derelict, *Bell* at Stilton (Fig. 84), another stone-built house inheriting Cotswold features.   That the English inn had gained a new status in the late sixteenth and seventeenth centuries can be best understood from the plays of Shakespeare and Ben Jonson.   Reference to inns, taverns and alehouses occur with frequency in the diary of Samuel Pepys, who knew the roads and the features out of London almost as thoroughly as Hobson the carrier knew the road between London and Cambridge.   From the diarist, Pepys, can be obtained the impressions he received when meeting King Charles the Second at Dover.   We think of the company at the Ship, the crowds on the foreshore watching the fleet standing in, as well as the anxiety of certain regicides who were anxious to quit the country before the excitement of the King's return had subsided.

It is to the gossipy secretary we are indebted for descriptions of food and bedding, of good and bad accommodation, observations noted down in that inimitable manner which allows the reader to expand the story. There is one passage which enables us to follow the diarist through the gardens of the Lion inn at Guildford and watch him cut the asparagus for his supper.   " They were the best that I ever ate in my life," he wrote, evidently with a moistening of the lips at the recollection.   To Samuel Pepys, no less than to Defoe and Izaak Walton, belongs the honour of leaving, not one, but many, short descriptions of late seventeenth century inn life.   There is Walton's description of the stuffed carp in the inn at Ware, surely the first of stuffed fish to grace the wall of an inn.

At the period after the Restoration the prosperity of the country is in the ascendant, the roads and the inns are busy.   The King makes frequent journeys to Newmarket and to Oxford with his courtiers. There are now many six-and eight-horse stage waggons, and at least six stage coaches, one of them scheduled " by the Grace of God " to run between London and Coventry by Dunstable and St. Albans.   In London, hackney coaches are licensed to ply for hire in the streets, and people are becoming favourable to the innovation of Sedan chairs.

The unimportant issues of the past contribute to the pageant which we view to such advantage and with such interest.   There is the enchantment of the distant view ; the coarseness then prevalent has in the passing of centuries become softened and mellowed.   The mundane details and trivialities have acquired that welcome cast of antiquity which makes us eager to note insignificant facts. Who, for example, during the Commonwealth was greatly concerned when the postal system was farmed out to John Manley, who used the chief inns as a part of his service ? The Post Office was evidently in a bad way at the Restoration, for improvements were suggested and acted upon, and for an annual rental of £21,500 the Duke of York eventually secured the control, doubtless for reasons of State and espionage. All credit is due to the stalwart William Dockwra, who in 1683 launched a metropolitan penny post, an event at that period almost as conspicuous as the rebuilding of St. Paul's Cathedral.

In any account of architecture, whether of inns, of private houses or public buildings, it is the contrasts that really matter, not so much the differences of mouldings and ornament as the never-ending change, the variety and the almost sub-conscious blending of old and new at the hands of the architects and craftsmen. Thus we find in Stuart and early Georgian days systems of building which are bound up with the essentials of the earlier tradition, methods of working in brick and stone, of plaster work and timber, tempered with a little classic learning of the delightfully dangerous kind. At the close of the seventeenth century, we find old inns undergoing further alterations, while new ones are building to meet the changing conditions of travel and commerce. Such of the London inns that had escaped the Great Fire were enlarged, while those destroyed in the local fires of Southwark and other parts of London were rebuilt. The roads at this time appear to some extent to have been improved, and travellers could consult their copies of Ogilby for a choice of routes. To this day can be seen the new inns of Queen Anne's reign, together with their successors those trim Georgian boxes of brick with sashed windows.

We have mentioned *The Haycock* at Wansford, as seen in Figs. 20-22, and we now refer to the older parts of *The George*, Stamford (Figs. 103, 104), and the Stamford Hotel (Fig. 116). In this category can be grouped *The Red Lion* at Truro, which Defoe knew almost as well as the inn at Brickhill, now in retirement as a farmhouse, which may well be the original named in " Moll Flanders." The country inns of the early eighteenth century were among the chief sights of England. Never did painted signs demonstrate such affection and loyalty to the monarch or such regard for the rights of the people. They became familiar in contemporary wood-cuts and novels ; while Addison wrote of signs and their faults, itinerant painters found a new means of existence, and it is evident that all kinds of craftsmen were called upon to show their skill in fashioning signs and supports which, modified to suit the new regulations in London, were subjected to no such restrictions further afield. Old views of the main street of Dartford in Kent (Fig. 190) and the High Street at Chelmsford in Essex (Fig. 198) show the extent to which signs were used. The early eighteenth century, therefore, became the new epoch of sign-making, for the signs were deemed as indispensable to the inn as the carved figurehead to the ship—the chief moral, the call to activity, to loyalty, emblems of the joy of living, coloured toys for grown-ups, in design as full of twirls, quips and jests as the period desired, and as florid in outline as the full-bottomed wigs which made all men appear of the same age. In the aspect of the taverns of this period is to be seen developed the spirit of freedom and merriment which graced the age of Elizabeth. From the architectural standpoint there is a difference—the outline of the Georgian inn was more severe, as were the windows, the assumed classicality of the mouldings and ornaments reflecting closer contact with the Continent. The inns of the period of transition, from Stuart to Queen Anne, include *The Saracen's Head* at Towcester, now *The Pomfret Arms* (Fig. 86), the inn at Tetsworth (Fig. 44), *The White Hart* at Whitchurch, and *The Castle* at Marlborough, the latter now part of the College.

There is no denying the pictorial qualities of the uniformed inns of the Hanoverian regime, rich in orange or plum brick with white paint trimmings. There are many which could be called venerable Uncle Tobies in the company of taverns. The majority are semi-official to outward appearance, but they show a tender regard for domestic felicity. In general, the inns built during the first quarter of the eighteenth century have a family likeness, but, as previously explained, the designs respond to regional conditions of material and craftsmanship. Many a hoary mediæal building was at this time subjected to a strait-waistcoat of red brick or grey stone, its old eyes were removed and new inserted, the bedrooms were extended into the ancient stabling at the back or alongside, new stairways were introduced to give access to odd corners, while the corridors at varying levels almost carry the road contours under the roofs—at least, so it appears to the unwary stumbling to bed by candlelight. We do not know the names of the builders who dressed up these delectable Georgian barracks; the little we know of the landlords is obtained from the billheads collected by Mr. Ambrose Heal. From the scratchings on the window-panes is revealed the disposition

of those who were not fastidious enough to conceal their thoughts or
their initials. The words "quaint" and "romantic" should have no
place in a description of realities, even although the identity of those
who once frequented these inns is lost beyond recall. Whither have
they gone, these "travaillers" and passengers who laboured from town
to town under many discomforts? They have left, it is true, the trace
of their passing, but the sun has gone for them; their world, too, has
passed, but we can still enjoy the warmth, colour and intricacy of the
material shell. Gone, too, are many of the stables, the horses, the
waggons, and the whole tribe of ostlers, chambermaids, landlords,
coachmen and guards. Where are the whips and the plated harness,
the heavy pistols and the battery of blunderbusses? The walls have
settled, the woodwork is worn smooth or polished to the tint of old ale
by coats of paint and varnish; the kitchens hold spits and cooking
utensils, now ornamental and unpolished; the vaulted cellars have
that damp earthy smell of double gloom, as though denied intercourse
with the outer world, for customs have continually changed with the
different attitude of men towards inns. Is it not strange that the inn
has passed through many vicissitudes and yet survives? It is no longer
a semi-official building, but a place of entertainment. No other country
can boast such diversity of building, or such variety of craftsmanship
—in short, such venerable indexes to social life as the inns of England.
Each inn epitomises history. And what of the landlords? Surely
some special corner of heaven has been allocated to the disciples of
St. Boniface, who in life were respected as postmasters and stage coach
proprietors. Did not the landlord own the line of stage waggons? Was
he not a figure at country fairs, courted by the squirearchy at election
times, unrivalled in his care of guests, renowned for his knowledge of
cooking, of wines, beer and humanity? This intimate and useful
system was doomed from the moment when James Watt toyed with
the kettle and saw a new power at hand.

We have paid many visits to *The White Horse* at Eaton Socon (Fig. 26)
on our journeyings between London and Edinburgh. Here is an inn
that fits in with the period of Smollett; indeed, it may well be the
identical house described by the novelist in "Sir Launcelot Greaves."
We searched for an inn of the period and selected the White Horse.
The house, built originally in the fifteenth century, was refronted at
the beginning of the second half of the eighteenth century. It has,
moreover, the especial interest of local associations. Samuel Pepys
frequently passed through Eaton Socon when The White Horse could

Fig. 15. A COMPANY OF PILGRIMS PASSING A
MEDIÆVAL CITY. (Early XVIth Century MS.)

Fig. 16. A MEDIÆVAL FIREPLACE.

Fig. 17. A XVIth CENTURY KITCHEN AND DINING-ROOM.
(From an engraving by J. B. Vries after P. Van der Borcht, illustrating a Biblical scene.

FIG. 18. OLD MEDIÆVAL GALLERY, ST. ALBANS.

FIG. 19 A MEDIÆVAL REMNANT OF THE GEORGE, HIGH STREET, BEDFORD.
(J. C. Buckler del 1837).

show externally its fifteenth-century framing.   Smollett must have known it soon after it had been refronted in brick.   Dickens, on the other hand, does not mention the name of the inn where the fellow-passengers of Nicholas Nickleby dined.

There is nothing more alluring than an attempt at reconstructing the scenes of other days.   If we view the interior of the principal room at The White Horse as it is with half-shut eyes, any part of the room assumes a different meaning.

It is a July evening of 1925 ; why not 1760 ?   The hour is seven, Let the years recede to suit our mood : have we not seen the letters and accounts of Bushmead Priory, the very secrets of the Geary family, the names of old servitors and locals to give reality to our musings ? We are for the nonce in telepathic communication with the old world. It is the hour of seven in the evening ; outside the inn the North Road stretches uninvitingly, for rain has fallen all day.   The floor is formed of large tiles scrubbed clean and sanded.   The chairs are of the spindled windsor type with Hogarth backs ; there is a panelled settle, some oaken stools and a " cricket " table.   At one side of the room is a deal dresser painted dark brown, garnished with pewter plates and dishes. The fireplace in the darkest corner is deep enough to hold two people on each of the recessed seats.   To the brickwork at the back of the fireplace is fastened a crane bearing a cauldron of stew, which is seething above the blaze of the sea-coal fire—a cheerful scene, every corner exercising its own peculiar spell, the company brought together by the chances of travel.   In a word, we are back in the York and London days.   This variegated view of the past is open to all ; to obtain it, it is not necessary to have been born an antiquary ; a similar view is open at any hostelry at any place and at any time.   Such impressions are momentary ; they are lost almost as quickly as they are gained, but the material facts of the inn remain.

During the second half of the eighteenth century the inn gradually improved.   The coach traffic could now be relied upon.   The " nobility and gentry " travelled in their own carriages.   There were regular stage-waggons to and from London, and others travelling on the cross roads.   The surface of the roads, it is true, left much to be desired, and we hear of one country gentleman in Devonshire who measured the ruts in order that the wheels of his new carriage should correspond in gauge.

People at this period, 1770, were rebelling against antique discomfort.   The rooms of the average inn were at this time panelled in deal, but the furniture in the best rooms was of mahogany. Hence it was that the curtains—rep and chintz—together with extra candles and the needlework bell-pulls, came to be charged in the bill. Oliver Goldsmith knew the value of a good marble mantelpiece to a landlord. It was at this time that travellers insisted on the use of the warming pan before venturing between sheets, and the " genteel " sort of people asked for silver etceteras to ornament the dinner table, to which custom can be attributed the Victorian demand for cruet money. The masters of the leading inns, many of whom were brewers and malsters, were the first to meet the demands for improvement, but the coaching inn did not attain its highest efficiency till the close of the reign of George III. It is significant that London led the way in almost every innovation, both in the sphere of travel and in the management of inns. It is to London we look for the semi-rural inns and pleasure gardens to which, on Sundays, the tradesman with his family made excursion.

The view of London of the second half of the eighteenth century can be widened by a study of the prints of Cheapside and other parts of the City. We have read Maitland and have looked through Dodsley. It only remains to visualise the aspect of London, let us say one Sunday morning in July, 1770. The day promises fair. Early as it is, the inn yards are peopled. Horses are attached to chaises and people are preparing to spend the day on the northern heights ; some incline to Richmond, to Hampton Court or Windsor. Being Sunday, no regular coaches are allowed on the road, except the long coaches to Greenwich, Blackheath and Croydon.

The holiday makers are mostly city apprentices, clerks and journey-men, with their womenfolk. We shall follow a party of six, with several small children, who have arranged themselves in a roomy chaise bound for Highgate, where they are due to dine at *The Gate House* at two o'clock.

London has enlarged some of its boundaries since the days of Queen Anne, and it is now a weekly occurrence for people of all classes who work within the city, from the cheesemonger to the printer's apprentice, to take their Sunday jaunts as a matter of course. It is a change, so runs general opinion, to get beyond crowded streets and away from petty worries, and the country is a greater attraction than the lions in the Tower menagerie. Newgate has many felons, but men and women are not hanged on Sundays. A visit to the northern or the southern heights enables people to look down on London, and there is the pleasure of locating the different wards and parish churches from a distance.

The chaise proceeds along Newgate Street, across Smithfield, and so to the village of Islington. The journeyman printer, at whose expense the party are being carried out of town, exclaims to his wife, "What a long way London stretches into the country ! Perhaps the day may come when the houses will reach to Highgate." His wife makes no reply to this absurd remark.

We leave the party at *The Gate House*, ready to explore the neighbourhood, much to the disgust of the gentry living in the Grove. We find the landlord and waiters at the Flask preparing tables for the ordinary, and similar preparations are being made at the Angel and the Wrestlers. There are Londoners racing their dogs, and below the crest of the hill is a man with a telescope who charges a penny a head for a peep at St. Paul's. On a week day, Highgate is almost as busy as the market-place of York ; on Sunday it is the cockney's turn to obey the call of the alluring village.

> " And many to the steep of Highgate hie,
> Ask, ye Boeotian shades, the reason why ?
> 'Tis to the worship of the solemn horn
> Grasped in the holy hand of mystery,
> In whose dread name both men and maids are sworn
> And consecrate the oath with draught and dance till morn."

Dinner over, the journeyman printer with other members of the party and chance friends elect to be sworn on the stag horns (Fig. 30), which distinguish The Gate House from the other inns. This ceremony takes place in the Assembly Room. The company is ready.

There is a thundering knock at the door, and in marches the Swearer, with a parson's gown and bands, wearing a mask and a full-bottomed wig like a judge's. The Clerk, wearing a verger's cassock, carries the horns fixed on a pole and a book to resemble the Bible.

The first candidate is called to the bar, and the oath delivered standing :—

The Swearer : " Take notice what I now say unto you, for that is the first word of your oath—mind that. You must acknowledge me to be your adopted father ; I must acknowledge you to be my adopted son (daughter). If you do not call me father, you forfeit a bottle of wine. If I do not call you son, I forfeit the same.

" And now, my good son, if you are travelling through this village of Highgate, and you have no money in your pocket, go call for a bottle of wine at any house you think proper to go into, and book it to your father's score.   If you have any friends with you, you may treat them as well, but if you have money of your own you must pay for it yourself, for you must not say you have no money when you have, neither must you convey the money out of your own pocket into your friends' pockets, for I shall search you as well as them, and if it is found that you or they have money, you forfeit a bottle of wine for trying to cozen and cheat your poor old ancient father.   You must not eat brown bread while you can get white, except you like the brown the best ; you must not drink small beer while you can get strong, except you like the small the best.   You must not kiss the maid while you can kiss the mistress, except you like the maid the best, but sooner than lose a good chance you may kiss them both.   And now, my good son, for a word or two of advice ; keep from all houses of ill-repute, and every place of public resort for bad company.   Beware of false friends, for they will turn to be your foes and inveigle you into houses where you may lose your money and get no redress.   Keep from thieves of every denomination.   And now, my good son, I wish you a safe journey through Highgate and this life.   I charge you, my good son, that if you know any in this company who have not taken the oath, you must call them to take it, or make each of them forfeit a bottle of wine, for if you fail to do so you will forfeit a bottle of wine yourself.   So now, my son, God bless you.   Kiss the horns or a pretty girl, if you see one here, which you like best, and so be free of Highgate."

Landlord : " Now, sir, if you please sign your name in that book ; if you can't write, then make your mark, and the Clerk of the Court will attest it.   You will now please to pay half-a-crown for Court fees, and what you please to the clerk."

We can imagine the ceremony to have been conducted with whimsical remarks, many a superfluous " Amen," and much laughter. At this period Highgate had many inns and taverns where it was possible to be sworn on the horns.   *The Gate House* was the most renowned.   *The Mitre, The Green Dragon, The Bell, The Rose and Crown, The Bull,* and *The Wrestlers* kept stags' horns ; *The Coach and Horses, The Castle, The Coopers' Arms, The Fox and Hounds,* and *The Angel* kept rams' horns, and *The Red Lion* kept bullocks' horns.

The custom of swearing on the horns seems to have been of ancient origin.   It may have originated amongst the graziers, for Highgate

FIG. 20. The Front.

FIG. 21 Back view.
THE HAYCOCK, WANSFORD, NORTHAMPTONSHIRE. An important inn of
the mid XVIIth Century, now a private house.

The Range of Stabling.

Fig. 22. The Sign.
THE HAYCOCK, WANSFORD.

being the place nearest the Metropolis where cattle from the north rested on their way to Smithfield, graziers were accustomed to stop for the night at one or other of the inns. Similar customs prevailed at Ware, Hoddesdon and Barnet. At Barnet there is still to be seen an inn with the sign of *The Hart's Horns*.

From 1790 onward many inns were remodelled. There are such examples as *The Dolphin* at Southampton, *Harker's* at York, *The White Hart* at Salisbury and new inns at Stockbridge, Bath and Bristol. From the literature of the time, as from the pencil of Rowlandson, and the brush of George Morland, much can be learned of the conditions of travel which, pleasant as it was in summer, was a form of penance in winter.

We pass from the closing years of the eighteenth century through the time of the struggle with Napoleon, bearing in mind De Quincey's enthusiasm for the mail coach, Washington Irving's pen pictures of English life, and the contemporary prints and drawings depicting the humours of the road, to view the inns and taverns of the year 1815. London is now a modern capital, new streets are being made in the City and in the West End, gas lighting is supplanting the oil lamps, the shops are as attractive as those of Paris, and road travel is at its zenith. Few, however, are aware that in twenty-five years the railways will change the existing order beyond recognition.

ROAD TRAVEL IN THE EARLY NINETEENTH CENTURY.

While certain engineers and inventors were giving attention to mechanical propulsion for road vehicles (Figs. 46, 48), the public remained content with horse traction. Heavy goods were conveyed by waggon (Fig. 34). The private carriage was the privilege of the rich. There was the post-chaise (Fig. 35) for those who could afford the expense, and the royal mail (Fig. 166) for professional people, or, failing that speedy conveyance, the much slower stage coach.

The second half of the eighteenth century had brought many changes. In 1815 we find not a few of the north-country coaches starting from the city and calling at the Peacock at Islington, the west-country coaches from the White Horse Cellar, or the Bear, in Piccadilly. The mail coaches set out from the old Post Office in Lombard Street. At this time it was possible to leave Newcastle on Monday morning and to reach London at five o'clock on the Wednesday morning following.

No better account of the discomforts of road travel is to be found than the following extracts from a contemporary dialogue between friends. The names of the friends have been changed to those of two descendants of the original speakers, and for the purpose of sequence we can imagine the dialogue to have taken place at the Sycamores, a private house at Highgate.

Mr. Hobson : " So here we are at last ! with the roof of a private house over our heads, and the free use of our own feet again for a month at least, I hope—bidding a long adieu to Bedlam in the shape of an inn, flying fields and trees under the name of prospects, wild beasts with saddles clapped on their backs—so-called horses—and a rattling trap for a sitting-room. For some time, at least, there is the pleasure of enjoying the amenities of Highgate."

Major Hanslip : " Well, Hobson, you are a skilful grumbler. For myself, I have a traveller's lumbago, the result of sitting twelve hours at a stretch, without being able to stretch."

Hobson : " Grumble, indeed ! It is a pleasure to sit by the fire and recount one's misadventures. Shall we ever forget the inn at Buckingham, where we were confined the whole day by the rain ? First we examined the window panes for curious verses and found nothing more piquant than :

' I love pretty Sally Appleby of Chipping Norton.'

' Sweet Dolly Meadows.'

' What better fair to think on
Than Nelly Proctor, toast of Lincoln ? '

Then we examined the wretched prints and wood-cuts, not a Morland nor a Rowlandson among them. O, those personifications of the Four Seasons, or the Cardinal Virtues, daubed over anyhow, with purple, red and raspberry cream colours, as well as the halfpenny prints ! I shall never forget the map of England with half the counties left out, and no towns in it, worked in a sampler by the landlady's youngest daughter, ' aged about ten years.' "

Major Hanslip : " O, horror, horror, horror ! Shall I add to your groans with my account of that wretched day ? "

Hobson : " Or that even worse time at the inn at Newark, when we shared a room and tried in vain to sleep on the assembly night, our chamber being immediately contiguous to the ball-room, and our ears assailed till the time of rising by the constant din of feet and fiddles, harp and pianoforte, not to mention the perpetual irruptions of whole herds of bucks blundering into the room, full of jest and roaring for refreshments. Neither was there lock nor bolt on the door."

Major Hanslip : " Perhaps you call to mind our arrival by post-chaise at Wymondham after a day's rattling, to say nothing of the window-glass in the chaise that could not be put down when it was up, nor up when it was down."

Hobson : " That was an experience. A poor reception at fair time, the only tolerable house being full, and we, perforce, having to take ourselves off to the worst inn and be shown into the worst room."

Major Hanslip : " Once I arrived at a lone inn, not on the late journey, with the intention of taking a bed, and found every room taken, so I had to pass a frosty night in a chair by the side of the kitchen fire, which was sullen and resisted all my abortive efforts to coax it into a blaze."

Hobson : " Have you ever tried to write in a stage coach ? The ancients could write on their tablets when travelling by chariot, at least I have read so in Melnoth's edition of Pliny."

Major Hanslip : " An impossible feat, even on a mail coach route."

Hobson : " Perhaps you will recall our experiences at Witham in Essex, where we arrived at the inn during a storm, half-drowned and half-frozen, in a calash."

Major Hanslip : " How eagerly we made for the kitchen fire, as being the warmest place, and how we were bumped, hustled, scalded and scolded by the mob of cooks and scullions who were getting the dinner ready ! "

Hobson : " But bad as the road is in winter and spring, it has its compensations in summer."

Major Hanslip : " O, those nights at inns ! No cards, no chess, only back gammon, and that generally played on a half-ruined board, half the men lost and no dice ! "

Hobson : " I have a grudge against bad inns, and especially do I long to punish landlords who cheat."

Major Hanslip : " Once at the Bell at Stilton " (Fig. 84), " I ordered some fruit for dessert. The bill was enormous and must have included the cost of repainting the sign, or at least the engraving of the sign on the bill-head." (See Figs. 4 and 5.)

Hobson : " Now you speak of exorbitant charges, don't you recall the terrible sandwiches at the Ram-Jam inn ? The bread thick, the butter bad, the mustard dirty, and only one inch of stale ham to four or five of stringy fat ? "

Major Hanslip : " That was an indigestible meal, but the jest of the sandwich is as old as the name of the noble earl who invented this form of spatchcocking meat within layers of bread."

Hobson : " O, those journeys by stage coach on the roads, with the wheels shrieking for grease, taking a hill at night at snail's pace with suspicious characters walking alongside, half one's wealth in the coach and only the rusty blunderbuss in the guard's hands to protect it ! "

Major Hanslip : " Give me a post-chaise and damn the expense. I am all for travelling in privacy. Think of the stings received from the various reptiles that swarm in and about stage coaches ! "

Hobson : " It is pitiful the way stage coaches are overloaded."

Major Hanslip : " It was a mean trick they played upon me at the Sugar Loaf at Dunstable when I went down to Brummagem in one of Sherman's heavy coaches from Lad Lane. The meal was delayed ten minutes out of the twenty we were booked to stop. When served, the soup was boiling, the outside passengers were snatching at loaves of bread, and just when the meat came in and I was hoping for something better, the coachman burst in with " All ready, Gem'men." When I returned to town and stopped at Dunstable, I took a round of beef in a dish from the sideboard into the coach and made sure of my meal, leaving it to the waiter to run half up the High Street for the reckoning."

Hobson : " What a dreadful time we had between Derby and Leicester ! "

Major Hanslip : " Bad, indeed, but not to be compared with entering a stage coach for a long journey, finding amongst other insufferables at least one muddling mother, with a sick but not silent infant, the windows all as close as wax for the poor child's sake."

Hobson : " Exasperating and trying for the nerves, but not to be compared to my journey to York in the mail coach, when I was whirled at breakneck speed through towns and picturesque scenes which I longed to sketch."

Major Hanslip : " O, the excitement of night travel, the vain attempts to sleep, the bumping of the head against the side panel while your other shoulder acts as a flying buttress to a snoring farmer ! The bumpings and the joltings, the shriek of the skidpan, your knees miserably cramped, your opposite neighbour a cramped old maid with piercing eyes, looking you through and through, the braying of the guard's horn, the feverish restlessness, and then the sudden halt in the wilderness, with twenty minutes for supper ! Out you get, yawning, limping, and shivering, trip up over the threshold, blunder down a dark passage lit by a candle held by the waiter, into a dark room where you sit in gloomy, weary, numb, stupid silence, waiting, it seems for ever, for the supper for which you have no stomach. A last bumper of negus, and out you are turned to face the night air, and back you creep into the interior of the travelling mousetrap, to the endless, hopeless racket and jumble."

Hobson : " Mail coaches, at any rate, are better than heavy lumbering stages, and the good inns are noted for their comforts."

Major Hanslip : " Mail coaches carry but five inside, and are not allowed by law to take more."

Hobson : " To add to our groans, now we are in comfort, don't forget the trip to Edinburgh from Manchester, through a variety of counties with which we were unfamiliar, when you discovered that you had left your itinerary of the roads behind, and we were at a loss to know the names of the villages and the seats of the nobility and gentry."

Major Hanslip : " That was a bad journey. We were frozen on the roof, and then had a pair of malefactors thrust upon us with the constables who were escorting them to Preston Assizes."

Fig. 24. THE TALBOT, OUNDLE, NORTHANTS.

Fig. 23. COURTYARD OF THE UNICORN, SHREWSBURY.

FIG. 25. TURPIN'S FETTERS, YORK.

FIG. 26.
THE WHITE HORSE, EATON SOCON, BEDFORDSHIRE.

Fig. 27. A Chimney Corner.

Fig. 28. A Panelled Settle.

THE WHITE HART, BLETCHINGLEY, SURREY.

Fig. 29.   MISERIES OF TRAVELLING: A HALT BY NIGHT.   1806.

SWEARING AT HIGHGATE.

Fig. 30.   SWEARING ON THE HORNS AT HIGHGATE.

Hobson : " My dear major, let us go no further with our reminiscences. We have spoken our hearts."

Major Hanslip : " It is almost decided that I must take charge of the new war prison at Norman Cross, so there is the end of my leisure on half pay. You, my dear Hobson, can come down within the day by the York Highflyer or the Stamford coach and stay in the vicinity. You will find plenty for your pencil among the French prisoners. For myself, I shall keep the Sycamores against a possible peace, for Bonaparte cannot keep up his present game. 'Twas a shrewd knock he recently got from Wellington in the Peninsula."

Hobson : " It will be good for all when the Continent quietens down. I have not been in Paris since the Peace of Amiens, but have had to content myself with sketching in England, and have even been suspected of spying for the French."

Major Hanslip : " The kettle is singing, so let us make the punch. The ladies are tired of our grumbling. I will retract all my animadversions. We have had our good days in the towns."

Hobson : " My sketch books are full. I shall approach Mr. William Miller of Albemarle Street, or Ballantyne of Edinburgh, with a view to the publication of the best of them to illustrate a book on the ' Delights of Travelling by Stage Coach.' Perhaps a future age will bring changes which will make our methods appear old-fashioned."

Another scene has been extracted from an early nineteenth century book, written about the time of the Battle of Waterloo. It describes the coffee room of the White Horse Cellar, Piccadilly, with travellers at various tables, waiters, servants, and friends of passengers.

A Traveller : " Waiter, waiter ! "—" Coming, sir ! "—" Make haste, do. I shall lose my place on the Bristol Mail."—" Very good, sir. Ten minutes yet, sir. Cut of roast beef, sir, potatoes and Yorkshire ? "—" Yes, that will do, but pray hurry, and bring some Harvey's Sauce."

Another Traveller : " Some table beer, please, and *do* hurry."

Voice Outside : " Any passengers for the Gloucester Mail ? "

Several Guests, excitedly : " One minute, one minute, we *must* pay the bill."

Voice Outside : " Can't wait. Time's up. I shall be brought to book if we're late."

Hasty exit of passengers, followed by waiter.

By the side of the coach :—

Fond Mother : " Tie a handkerchief around your neck, William, and mind you give my love to grandpa. Good-bye, my love."

The Guard : " All right."

The Coachman : " Let 'em go."

On the coach :—

Wounded Officer : " You have a strange crowd on board."

Coachman : " They wary from day to day, sir, They're lively now, but once off the stones they'll settle down."

The coach jolts and bumps out of London, through Brentford, Colnbrook, Henley and Maidenhead. The day wears on, until at midnight such of the passengers as have booked through stop at *The New Inn* at Gloucester.

We are not so far removed from the early nineteenth century to have lost touch with the incidents of inn life and road travel. Butterfly coaches are still to be seen on the roads, and such do not look out of place, and the inns of the Pickwickians are still functioning. While at Harwich we had the good fortune to peruse an account of inn life written by a visitor from Holland who came to these shores a few months after Waterloo. It is a somewhat lengthy description, but it has the value of describing the smallest details of the inn and the subsequent journey to town.

The Dutch visitor arrived at *The White Hart,* Harwich, after a rough passage in the sailing packet, and he was struck with the welcome and the superior accommodation of the inn. He writes :—

" I have just landed and have been shown into The White Hart inn. The boatswain has returned to the packet for my luggage, which is to get to the Customs House. First, I will breakfast, and then view the town. I ring the bell and a person dressed like a gentleman comes in. He is of enormous bulk—a typical John Bull. I make this man a bow, taking him for the host, and dismiss him to send a waiter to me. ' I am the waiter, sir,' he replied. He then disappeared, and within five minutes served up a most elegant breakfast. There was a teapot of a kind of black earthenware, which I have since learned to be of Wedgwood make, with a low relief of classic figures ; the cream pot was of silver, the cup and saucer of Staffordshire ware, but, oh, how large the cup ! The tea-caddy was of neat lacquer work, and, in the divisions, I found excellent green and black tea with a scalloped silver spoon for ladling out the exact measure. There was a china plate with toast, top and bottom, upon a china bason, and another with slices of thin bread and butter, also a bason of very fine loaf suger. All this was brought to me on the neatest tray. I made the tea myself to my taste. Another waiter then brought in a copper scuttle shaped like a Roman helmet. I felt very comfortable, such was the elegance of the fireplace, the polished steel grate, the fender of polished steel, and the

FIG. 31.   THE GEORGE, GRANTHAM.

FIG. 32.   THE EAGLE YARD, CAMBRIDGE.

Fig. 33. PACKHORSES.

Fig. 34. LOADING A HEAVY WAGGON.

Fig. 35. LOADING A CHAISE. (From Aquatints by J. B. Pyne.)

poker, shovel and tongs, with vase tops, with which it was such a delight to stir the fire.

"I had leisure to inspect the private room. It was spread with a pretty carpet worked to a uniform pattern, with a large White Hart at the centre. Breakfast over, I asked to be shown to my bed-chamber. There I found comfort and elegance. A carpet covered the centre of the floor, on which stood a mahogany bed with a painted cornice and dainty curtains, and a most wholesome counterpane as white as snow, with a beautiful design of flowers. On the right was a bow-fronted mahogany chest of drawers with a stand glass of the finest workmanship upon it ; on the left, a closed-up wash-hand stand with blue Staffordshire jug and bason ; at the side was a towel-horse with two towels neatly folded. The sash windows were hung with dimity, and besides, had white blinds to be let up or down at will. There were two light chairs with cane bottoms, a night-stool and a small table for writing. The fireplace had a hob grate with two figures, one on either side, cast with the metal. What a contrast to the hotels of my own country, where everything is so antique ! Oh, I thought, if the rooms of the public inns are like this, what must the apartments of the nobility be like !

"Well satisfied, I gave notice of my intention of spending the rest of the day in seeing the town. Dinner was on the table when I came back, but soup and table napkins I did not see. The waiter, the fat one, did stare when I asked for these, but it appears that the White Hart did not understand my wants, so I was forced to use my handkerchief. But the table was crowded with things. It had a cotton cloth, quite clean, and many utensils which looked like silver, including an epergne with glass dishes in which were grapes, apples and sweetmeats. There was an immense joint of roast beef at the head of the table, and a leg of mutton of equal bulk at the bottom, both awaiting and defying the guests. The table was set for ten persons, and each set of knives and forks was flanked with two different sorts of fruit pies. There were two large dishes of potatoes, and French beans, and wedged among these was a mahogany waggon in which rode an enormous Cheshire cheese. With the potatoes was butter sauce, and in glass jars I did notice some pickled onions and some walnuts, which gave a particular relish to the beef. The company being seated, we fell to. For drink, there was London porter, and for wine, some port, which I found to be mixed with brandy. The meal over, three waiters appeared and whipped the cloth from over our heads. It was done so dexterously that no one seemed to mind. Then they brought on the dessert—grapes, walnuts, apples—and crackers, with a special service of highly decorative plates, as well as napkins of checked pattern, evidently of wool, which were of no use, and so with eating, drinking and talking, the time did pass till tea was ready, and there was no great difference between this meal and my breakfast. Then at nine o'clock, being tired, I retired to my bed-chamber with a plated candlestick I had seen outside on a table in the corridor, awaking next morning to find my boots jet black with some polish, and so again I took my breakfast in the private room and prepared for my journey to London. The bill was most reasonable, amounting to some twenty-six shillings per day, including the service, but I was perturbed at the number of persons who came with me to the door—the cook, the chamber-maid, the under-waiter, the head-waiter, the boots—all claiming a fee. I got rid of this legion for ten shillings. The coachman, he asked the guard if all was right, and then we started on the great road. On the right and left as we passed along I noticed country houses of brick, with neat gardens. There were orchards and wheat and turnip fields. People all appeared plump and well-fed, the children being very attractive. There was a vast number of private carriages and post-chaises, as well as elegant gigs on the road. One thing struck me in particular ; it was the neatness of the fences and the gates, as well as the design of the toll-houses and the turnpike gates, all of which were painted in white. We stopped at Colchester, at Chelmsford and at Brentwood, and so came into London by Romford, Stratford-le-Bow and Whitechapel, the houses in this part appearing exceptionally old."

A clearer account of the typical English inn as it appeared a little more than a century since could not have been written. At this time there was no idea that coaching or road travel could possibly end, yet within the next thirty years the industry that gave employment to thousands was practically extinct.

A letter from an early Victorian lady to her cousin is illuminating on this point, for it describes a journey from Chippenham to London, which was something of an adventure.

"January 25th, 1844,
"Thomas's Hotel, Berkeley Square.

"My Dear Kathleen :

"You will see that I have arrived in town, after an adventurous journey by road. My state of mind would not permit me to travel by rail, for Mr. Brunel is no hero of mine, since he has destroyed posting, put down coaches and compelled people to sit behind his puffing

FIG. 36. TYBURN TURNPIKE, ABOUT 1830. (G. Shepherd, del.)

FIG. 37. A COUNTRY TOLLGATE. (J. B. Pyne, del.)

FIG. 38. THE ELEPHANT AND CASTLE, ABOUT 1780. (T. Rowlandson del.) (*v. also Fig.* 138.)

FIG. 39. CHANGING HORSES. (J. Pollard del.)

FIG. 40.   THE TURK'S HEAD, ALDGATE HIGH STREET, LONDON, E.
(J. T. Wilson del. 1869.)

FIG. 41.   A DERELICT BEDROOM IN THE COCK, TOTHILL STREET,
WESTMINSTER, ABOUT 1850.   (J. W. Archer, del.)

FIG. 42. THE INN IN DECAY: THE OXFORD ARMS, WARWICK LANE,
ABOUT 1870.   (v. also Fig. 149)

monsters. Two days have passed since Belinda and I left our home.
Tom was so infatuated with the idea of going first class on the Great
Western that I decided to give him the entire charge of the trunks;
he is now in Hertfordshire with the Thorntons. You could not imagine
that we two women were allowed to take a lengthy journey on deserted
roads with the bare possibility of getting horses. I had hoped that we
should make London before night, but there was always the possibility
of a fog. Just think of the awful risk of damp beds, and no one sleeps
at inns since the railway has been cut. 'We sha'n't get to Reading
before three, unless we get horses,' said Belinda as we seated ourselves
in the barouche, 'and we shall certainly have to sleep on the road.'
We admired the country, noted the heavy frost, and talked over our
neighbours' affairs until we came to the end of the first stage, a dull-
looking village, eleven miles from home. We drew up at *The Golden
Lion*, which ten years since was one of the busiest inns on the road.
The inn looked deserted—no ostler, no horses ready saddled as in the
times when we were children and landlords took a real pride in their
stables. We looked at each other in consternation. 'Any horses?'
shouted Richard. The landlady, a slatternly person in curl-papers,
came out in a slipshod way. 'No,' was plainly written on her face.
She seemed surprised to see an old-fashioned travelling carriage and
four. 'No, milady, we are new people. We are just come into the
house. The people afore us was ruined; since the railroad came this
way nobody wants horses.' 'Will you please to unlight, if you please,
milady,' said the elder postilion, a man of about fifty-five, still called
a boy; 'we'd take you on another stage if so be you'd bait an hour.
The horses would be fresh enough.' 'Ay, sure sartin, ma'am,' inter-
polated the younger postilion, 'the 'orses could take you two stages
more, if so be you'd bait an hour.' There was no alternative, so we
descended and followed the landlady into the guest room. I looked
around at the desolate room while the woman went off for chairs, and
noted the old bell pulls which seemed to have become melancholy since
the Bristol mail was stopped. How different it would have been ten
years since! The hour passed, and once again we took our seats, this
time not so excitedly. We were now on the worst stage, a particularly
hilly one, and the surface of the road had been neglected by the
turnpike trust. 'Ah,' thought I, 'they will never make another
cutting, they will not undertake systematic levelling or throw another
bridge across a hollow. Thirty years from now the roads will be as
bad as they were in our grandfathers' days, that is, if the world does

not come to an end. And who will inherit these decayed hostelries?
Who will look at the ruined villages, the moth-eaten hangings and
the rusty grates?' So we jogged on to the end of the next stage. We
stopped only a few yards from another inn, the Red Lion. Here we found
slightly better comfort, for the inn is on a cross route and still boasts
a two-horse coach, and we were fortunate enough to secure a change of
horses which carried us to Newbury, where we made a halt until further
horses could be obtained from a livery stable. On, once more, two
stages to Reading, and then another change. The light was failing, what
with delays and bad cattle, it was dark when we drew near a small
tavern eight miles beyond. The inn in the village seemed busy enough;
the landlord said it was a great struggle to keep things going, but he
protested on the cleanliness of his rooms and the aired state of his beds.
With wondering steps we followed the woman-waiter upstairs into
the bedroom and waited in misery while she lit the fire. The woman
said it was 'the worst grate in the house, only arter a bit it would burn
up.' It was cold comfort for two women, who had spent the day under
such difficulties. The woman-waiter was exceedingly noisy, and the
wind rattled the casements and blew the smoke down the chimney.
We made preparations for dinner, and on this being announced we
made our way to the coffee room. Fortunately no other travellers were in
the inn, but there were several gentlemen's servants staying in another
part of the house who had been sent by their masters up to London
by road. We found an old-fashioned mahogany table in the centre
of the coffee-room large enough to hold twenty. There was a sideboard
covered with all sorts of utensils that bumped, rattled and shook like
one of Mr. Brunel's trains every time the woman-waiter stamped about.
At last came the mutton, smoking hot and tender, followed by a pudding
tasting strongly of onions. This dinner, such as it was, compensated
for all the injuries we had gone through, and so, as Mr. Cunningham
tells us, or makes Pepys tell us, we went to bed, when we found the
fire at last red hot. So we fell to playing backgammon, twisting the
dice box and pausing ever and anon to listen to the whistling of the
wind that must have taken off a tile at every gust. Next morning
we packed into the barouche and in three stages reached London, not
experiencing any difficulty with horses. We came by way of Brentford
and the back streets of Fulham and Chelsea, driving through Albert
Gate and out of Stanhope Gate, much to the astonishment of some
men of fashion who must have been exceedingly surprised at our mud-
stained, old-fashioned travelling coach. And so we are in Berkeley

FIG. 43. HALF MOON, BURY ST. EDMUNDS.

FIG. 44. THE SWAN, TETSWORTH, OXFORDSHIRE.

FIG. 45. A HUNT SUPPER. (H. Alken, del.)

Fig. 46.   GURNEY'S STEAM CARRIAGE, 1827   (G. Scharf del.)

Fig. 47.   THE FALMOUTH MAIL LOADING UP, ABOUT 1830.

FIG. 48. A " BONESHAKER."

FIG. 49. THE EPPING HUNT, OR HOBBIES IN AN UPROAR.

Square. Think of it! we have defied Brunel, Stephenson and Hudson, the railroad kings—two defenceless women suffering from nerves and the fear of damp beds, footpads and weak horses, travelling ninety miles by road in the old manner, when everything goes at thirty miles an hour by steam.

" Ever your loving friend,
" Marjorie St. Aubyn."

In the 'forties of the last century it is evident that roads were fast falling into decay. The early experiments with steam coaches had failed, for the innovation of the railroad and the seemingly incredible speed of the locomotive had captured public imagination. It was the period of decline. During the next thirty years the roads and the inns are to fall into even a worse state (Figs. 41-44), but the sporting instinct of Englishmen, the love of the road and the feeling for antiquity, which is a national trait, never quite allowed the respect for what had been to pass away. We find the engineers still busy with ideas to make steam-driven road carriages and the legislature as busy to keep them in check with legal formalities and red flags. We find enthusiasts making long tours in dogcarts, during the 'fifties and 'sixties. There are sporting contests between University undergraduates to see how fast a horse will trot between shafts ; trotting championships, and meets of the four-in-hand clubs. By and by the unwieldy boneshaker (Fig. 48) makes its appearance and the riders are greeted with abuse and showers of stones. Then come the spirited young men of the 'sixties, who, wearied of the railway, strapped haversacks on their backs and made a fashion of the six weeks' walking tour. Meanwhile, interest in the coaching days is fostered by a hundred pens. Eventually, in 1871, we meet Mr. Edwards and his mule cart setting out from Aldgate Pump in quest of inns.

London in the 'seventies had changed but little from late Georgian times. There are many new buildings in the City. There are lines of omnibuses and horse-drawn tramcars through north and east London. There are business men living out of town who make the journey into the City daily by rail. Interest in the inns is about to revive. There are one or two solitary coaches on the road, mainly butterflies. Every night at ten of the clock or a little before, heavy postal and parcel wagons, with lamps ablaze, leave the yard of St. Martin's le Grand for Bedford, Oxford, Cambridge and the home towns of Kent, Essex, Surrey and Buckinghamshire. They pass on to the high roads through the gaslit streets, almost unnoticed by the mass of people. Yet these lumbering vehicles are survivals of road travel, the slight links in the chain of tradition that bind the past to the revival which has come about in our own time. The old inns of the road are in process of being modernised, not always happily, as in the case of *The Rose and Crown* at Saffron Walden, which had the good luck to be attended to by Eden Nesfield. It is the age when City men drive tandem dogcarts in emulation of Guards officers, and it is almost impossible to distinguish the travelling bagman, in his smart buggy with the hood, from the country doctor. They have left their traces in the contemporary numbers of " Punch," and are remembered by the drawings of Du Maurier, of Harrison Weir and Randolph Caldecott. It is not strange that the late Victorian period should have shown an unwillingness to part too speedily with tradition and that through the work of a few artists and the labours of Kate Greenaway, as well as that of the architects, the modern spirit in domestic building should have had its beginning. The truth is that there is no abrupt change, only slow evolution with tradition as the keynote. Hence it is that interest in the road, the inn, and English travel, in spite of the railroad with its set rules, by-laws and conventions, did not bring about the entire demolition of the English respect for old customs. This island is not a large one, and to-day we travel almost as fast by road as Victorians did by rail. The inns, however, for the most part remain untouched. The roads have been levelled, one would almost say ruled, and if the fare of the inns does not reach the high status of the palmy days of coaching, it is improving ; but there is still need for reform in the matters of entertaining and feeding of guests. The Victorian hotel at this time was springing up in all sorts of places, in town as in the country, it was a feature of Victorian enterprise and a novelty to the visitors who annually spent their holidays at the seaside. We will not waste time on it, for it may still be seen in its splendour. If there is one man of the time to whom a monument is due, or at least recognition in the pages of the Dictionary of National Biography, that man's name is Edwin Edwards, the pioneer of modern interest in the subject of inns. This author started out to etch the inns of England at a time when most persons were thinking such places were obsolete institutions. Edwards' idea was to record the most interesting examples remaining on the old coach roads, a subject consistent in all literature from Chaucer to Hogarth, Smollett, Wilkie, Dickens and Thackeray. As member and president of the Hogarth Club, Edwards was especially fitted for the task. We find in his etched work and his slight line representations a freedom of expression as well as a love of the subject he essayed. His book and his plates are eloquent of the inns and the roads which he rediscovered out of London. It was his proposal to separate England and Wales into the four cardinal divisions of East, West, North and South, and to devote two parts to each part of each division. But the task was beyond his strength, and although the eastern part was almost complete, and he had collected material for the northern and southern sections, he did not live to see the massive volume which appeared in 1880. But in the preface he had prepared he records the labours of his printer for the general get-up, and immortalises his mule's death, the patient supplier of tractive forces who drew him along the road on the " outs for inns."

We give some extracts from a letter written by Edwards to his friend.

" The Inn at Scole, Norfolk,

" *17th of August*, 1871.

" My Dear Morrison

" The pleasures of leaving and coming back to London are many, for the Metropolis is a good place to live in, if only for the delight of getting out of it. As you are already aware, I anticipate such pleasures for some years in continually going from and coming back to this endless region of brick and mortar. I propose to etch by the way all characteristic examples of old inns that remain, and to confine myself for the most part to the old, and now almost deserted, turnpike roads. You will see that we are now well on our way into the heart of East Anglia, independent of the Great Eastern line, and travelling behind a mule who seems to love me as I love her, dearly. By my side, on the front seat of a little rattle-trap phaeton, sits the best companion that a man can have, a wife. In the back seat I have my luggage, my etching plates and guide book. There is also an old copy of Patterson's ' Roads,' the nineteenth century edition by Mogg (the Bradshaw of old coaching days). I determined to go to East Anglia by Whitechapel and come back by Shoreditch, thus covering the two mail coach routes given in Patterson. First we halted at Aldgate Pump, that vantage spot from where people, from time immemorial, have started to walk round the world, and from whence, even now, market porters race with six baskets on their heads to Covent Garden for a wager. I stopped Jet while I had a draught from the pump in memory of the venerable Stow, and then

into Whitechapel.   As we proceeded the road gradually widened.   I
was astonished at the number of butcher's shops, and it dawned upon me
that this quarter must be one of the largest depôts in London for the
sale of dead meat.   In the middle of the road stood a long row of hay
carts from Essex, so I concluded it to be the haymarket of East London.
We clip-clopped on the granite to Whitechapel church, the standard
measuring point for the eastern road.   Its large, round windows seemed
to indicate that we were then at zero, and near this I stopped again to
talk with the driver of an omnibus waiting here to start his journey
cityward.   This obliging man pointed out the exact spot of the original
turnpike which, with its white lodges, has long since been removed.
Here is a sample of his conversation written down almost exactly.
' Do I recollect the old coaching days ?   Lord bless you ! how old do you
think I am ?   Why, I can recollect well enough the illumination for
Queen Caroline when boys in the streets ran about with placards,
shouting " Long live Queen Caroline ! " and them as didn't illuminate
had all their windows smashed.   Lord, the sight of four-in-hand coaches
as used to drive through the old gates here every day !   Such spankin'
fine teams, all four horses matching to a hair, the last stage into London
and the first out was always horsed the best, leastways for show.   Such
whips, such drivers, the country don't produce now ! '   We continued
our way eastward down Mile End, past the Trinity Almshouses, which
some say were designed by Wren (though how he found time for the
work passes comprehension), and so on to the borders of Essex.   We
soon cleared of this mighty mass of bricks and mortar, of smoke and
shipping, and crowds of hurrying people, and passed into the green
fields.   There, on our right, could be seen the distant blue hills of Kent,
and, on our left, the long, lofty woodlands that mark all that is left
of the Hainhault and Epping Forests.   The inns became detached,
the villas gave place to neat country boxes of Georgian lines standing
in their own grounds, like gentlefolk aloof at an assembly, and so on
through the brickfields of Ilford and the market gardens, meeting from
time to time droves of Essex calves and noting the wood-built solitary
houses of the jobbing gardeners.   On and on, with plenty of etching
subjects suggesting themselves, until we entered the broad market place
of Romford, and passing through, after a brief halt, we reached Brentwood, where, having accomplished eighteen miles of our journey, we put
up for the night.   *The White Hart,* where we inned, seems fairly to hold
its own among the great changes in the system of locomotion.   Strange
it is that relays of post horses are still to be had at this inn, with aged

FIG. 50.   THE DUKE OF YORK, POTTER'S BAR.
(Early XVIIIth Century.)

FIG. 51.   SIGN OF THE RED LION, BARNET.

FIG. 52. The Front.

FIG. 53. The Seat in the Yard.
THE GEORGE, BUCKDEN, HUNTINGDONSHIRE.

post lads, one of whom told us that many of the gentry hereabouts still decline to travel to town by the rail, but ride post in their own carriages to and from London.   As far as I can gather, The White Hart seems to be the favourite sign in Essex, more so than in any other part of England. Brentwood has always been famous as a resting-place for travellers. We were shown into an old-fashioned coffee-room for supper and then obtained a delightful bedroom.   The next morning I examined the wheels of the phaeton, patted Jet affectionately as I harnessed her to the shafts, and with my dear wife at my side, again took to the road.   On we went, through the undulating country to Chelmsford, now trotting and now walking, looking at tiled roofs and weather-boarded houses, at neat brick fronts and delicate doorways.   I would that some of our modern houses looked as sweet.   We took our time, resting to eat and apply the needle on the copper plate, endeavouring to catch impressions of old signs, curious roofs and overhangs.   You shall read all about Chelmsford and other details when the book is published.   From Chelmsford we decided to go on as far as Scole Inn, our present address, by way of Braintree, Sudbury and Bury, and later to resume our route to Yarmouth by way of Colchester and Ipswich, and Chelmsford afterwards, for I learned that Witham is a place to see and that *The White Hart* in that town is noted for its antiquity.   Everywhere I find signs of the industrious Flemings, who settled in these parts during the reign of Queen Elizabeth and introduced their woollen manufactures and occupied the inns.   After several halts we reached Sudbury, the large, old-fashioned, straggling clothing town.   I selected a corner post of the old inn as a subject for the needle, and while engaged in my work I was asked by an admiring spectator, ' Did you know that in the house next the inn there was a man lived who was very famous about two hundred years ago for wood-carving ?   I think Simon Sudbury was his right name. He fell in love with a daughter of a rich wool stapler who lived in that house, but the wool stapler would have nothing to say to him because he was poor.   So Master Simon, he came to London. St. Paul's Cathedral was then a-building, and this here Sudbury tried to get some work there.   None of the men would give him a job, so what did he do but set to and done a carving of an old sow with a litter of pigs. He looked out for his chance and put himself and his sow and his pigs in the way of Sir Christopher Wren when he was looking over St. Paul's with a lot of ladies.   Sir Christopher was so pleased with his carving that he gave him plenty to do in St. Paul's, which is full of his work to this day.   He came back to Sudbury very rich, married the wool stapler's daughter, and lived and died in that same house. All the carvings in it were done by him.'

" I asked my informant what authority there was for his story. He said that ' there was a letter in the British Museum that proved every word of it.' And so the day passed. We reached Bury that night, and the next day arrived at Scole, where we intend to stay, as I consider this to be the most remarkable inn in the country.

" Ever your sincere friend,

" EDWIN EDWARDS."

Nine years later, 1880, Mrs. Ruth Edwards writes :—

" To-day, nine years after our first journey in quest of inns, I have seen the first copy of the great work projected by my dear husband. The companion of his toil, I remain the solitary servant of his fame, and of the several duties he bequeathed to me for my future occupation none has seemed to me more urgent, indeed, nor is likely to prove more congenial, than the task of enlarging the reputation of the work by which he is, for the present, chiefly known among artists."

From the early 'eighties onwards the cycling boom rose to its height, and many will remember the aspect of the metropolis at that time : London gay with its freshly painted stucco, garden-seated omnibuses and tickets in exchange for pence ; the smoky underground rattling from the City to Baker Street, with extensions to outlying suburbs ; the trams horse-drawn, with the exception of the cable systems on Highgate Hill and through Streatham. There were one or two services of long distance 'buses making a journey of eight miles into the umbrageous greenery of the home counties. There was virgin country at Golders Green, with haymaking in progress ; the roads were thronged with cyclists, mostly proud possessors of machines with pneumatic tyres, with here and there an old-fashioned ordinary and a still more antiquated tricycle. There were a few motor cars of curious shape, the Benz and the Panhard predominating. The latter were looked upon with contempt by the cyclists, who had no difficulty in outdistancing the unreliable automobiles. Even near London the inns displayed notices offering roadside accommodation, heralding the coming revival of inn-keeping. As we recall this particular morning, there were four-horse brakes loaded with trippers going to Hadley Woods, Epping Forest and other parts ; with four-horse pleasure coaches on the roads to Hertford and St. Albans, to Windsor and Oxford. But these coaches are strange butterflies.   The painted signs of the Cyclists' Touring Club and the Cyclists' Union were then conspicuous on the dangerous hills ;   the roads for the most part had splendid metalled surfaces, for the surveyors were keen wheelers.   Some cyclists indulged in speed, and police traps were working for the suppression of road racing, for the police had not been educated to anything that moved faster than a horse or the steam roller advancing like a juggernaut behind a red flag.

The 'nineties of the last century now seem remote.   London has since developed into the best parts of the adjacent counties and now threatens to extend its ribbons even further afield, but time has worked its revenge on the railways and has once again brought the road into favour.   We have to look upon the last years of the nineteenth century as providing an interlude to the present.   It was the bicycle that caused the roads and the inns of the past to be revived.   Then was reinstituted the call of the country, the feeling akin to independence and consequence which arose from holiday tours.   It is surprising how slowly innovations are accepted.   As early as 1820 the hobby horse (Fig. 49) and tricycles of sorts were on the roads and became subjects for caricature ;   but it was not until the 'seventies that the idea of propulsion by human power entered upon its final stages.   Since then cycling has become general and is now in process of being overshadowed by the motor car. The early days of cycling were pleasant, the inns were revisited after fifty years of neglect ;   old people, landlords, ostlers and postboys were discovered who remembered the St. Martin's summer of the coaching era.   It was sufficient then, after a journey on dusty roads, to be content with little accommodation, to rest contented and to survey the old relics in comparative privacy.   Just as Kate Greenaway viewed the picture of the early nineteenth century and recast her impressions into the drawings which delighted us as children, so the tourist of the 'nineties was brought face to face with unspoiled survivals of the road.   Those were sunny moments on the pilgrimage of life's way, then were sketch books produced and pencils active ;   cyclists were the Alexander Selkirks of the road, seeing all and harbouring memories.   We remember once talking to an old bootmaker who had made a pair of Wellingtons for the driver of a coach on the Cambridge Road.   It was oddly enough within the diminutive parlour of a small tavern.   The old fellow's thoughts were in the past, he lolled in his elbow-chair, and his eyes had a far-away look as he described the spanking teams, the brightly painted coach and the way it kept scheduled time past his workshop.   He was almost garrulous on the subject and gave us to understand that he had never travelled on the railway; but when he spoke his eyes flashed and we could see the strength of his respect for the vanished days. It has taken over a century to produce the bicycle and to perfect the motor car. There were times in the last century when the trunk roads were practically deserted, indeed one would have thought that the inventive powers of the Victorians might have at least concentrated on steam coaches. It is difficult to state the exact year in which the idea of a steam coach was first hit upon. James Watt invented a steam engine in 1784, which he suggested might possibly be found useful in moving ordinary vehicles along the road, but his theory was allowed to lapse. The next inventor was Richard Trevethick, who constructed a steam carriage in 1798. His first road machine was ready in 1801. In 1803 Trevethick tested his carriage in Oxford Street. All traffic was stopped while the lumbering vehicle, belching smoke from its stack, made its way over the stones at ten miles an hour. Other inventors followed the lead of the Cornishman; they include the names of Major Pratt, John Stevens, William Palmer, Thomas Tindall, W. Brunton, Joseph Reynolds, David Gordon, Julius Griffiths, Burstall of Edinburgh, and J. Hill of London. Burstall's carriage was a veritable juggernaut, which weighed eight tons and failed for want of power to move its mass. By 1829 the construction of steam carriages had reached the practicable stage (Figs. 46 and 172). It was then that W. H. James of Holborn produced his steam coach, which ran from London to Stratford at fifteen miles an hour. Then followed ideas of the pilot wheel for steering, as shown in Hancock's steam carriage, Dr. Church's steam coach, which ran between London and Birmingham, and Gordon's steam carriage. Sir Goldsworthy Gurney built a steam carriage in 1828 which seemed to have solved the problem at this date (Fig. 46). It ran for four consecutive months, four times a day over an ordinary country road nine miles long without a single accident, and it carried, during this time, three thousand passengers about four thousand miles. We are told the time taken for the trip was about forty-five minutes. Steam coaches, however, were far from popular. The coaching public were dead against such contraptions, and the passing of the "Turnpike Act" stopped the enterprise for nearly seventy years.

The motor car, which must be regarded as the successor of the bicycle, has brought the inn almost to the status of its old prosperity, but with this exception—there is no regular traffic to be catered for. So swift is road travel to-day that the map of England appears almost insignificant. It is common for tourists to make a journey from London to Scotland by motor coach, and for individual motorists to undertake lengthy journeys within the day which would have seemed incredible to their ancestors.

There are some who are still content with more leisurely going, and to these the inns have a special attraction. We are begininng to enquire into the architectural secrets, to find out the names of inns that have been changed into farmhouses and private residences. We find most of the old inns to be stored with relics and curiosities, and we no longer have the easy faith to be deceived in such matters. As we journey we try to piece together the story, to gather the innocuous tavern rhymes, or ascertain which is the loneliest or the highest inn in the country, or search for mural tablets to the memory of innkeepers. There is such a monument in the church at Brickhill on Watling Street. It is a pleasant pastime gathering traditionary anecdotes and attempting to bridge the long period when the inns were in partial decay. The subject is endless and never tires. The innkeepers have responded to the revival of road travel in a way befitting their calling. At some inns the tradition has never lapsed, nor a shadow allowed to spread itself over the house. There is no keener conservator of the past nor saner custodian of antiquity than a proud landlord of an historic inn. He is a churl among innkeepers who will not show his house or has no soul above the presenting of a bill. With what care are preserved the time-tables of the crack coaches, the forgotten bills of fare, the printed accounts of pugilistic contests, races and elections. In one house will be seen a framed letter from a royal equerry, in another, a letter from Dickens, in another, a quotation from Shakespeare. At *The Lamb Inn*, Hartley Row, can be seen a print of Gay's verse describing the road to Exeter and the halt at the Lamb. It is from such relics that we gain our knowledge at firsthand of the privileges of inns, which we verify from Pepys, Farquhar, Smollett and Dickens. There are the visitors' books, the autographs on the window panes, the display of plate, the sporting prints, and the impedimenta of the house to help our devotion. Then, how strangely the design of the automobile fits in with the old setting of an inn courtyard. The shapes of the closed cars are strangely reminiscent of the post-chaise; the open car has something of the form of the curricle and the calash—only the horses are lacking.

In the evolution of a century many new things seem to revert to a resemblance of the earlier forms from which they have sprung. To have the feeling of the past, one must make long stays at inns. What else are these venerable houses ; if they fail to please by their associations, have they any other meaning than that of traditional sequence and pictorial charm ?   They have the true lineage of antiquity, detaining us by the welcome look of their externals and receiving us within the time-worn walls as though we were erring prodigals.   It is not so much the fact that by paying the bill we can obtain food and rest, as it is the privilege of being able to command them for our temporary enjoyment.   We enter the inn light-heartedly, living again in the past, poring over the details which seem in their amazing age to be endowed with perpetual vitality.   We greet each oddity of the house like some old friend, and feast our eyes on the light and shade as though the perspective would never tire.   The experiences of one day will be different the next.   It is a pastime few can resist.   Company and conversation is never lacking at an inn.   At the fireside in winter, or in the garden when the weather is fair, there is always something to enliven and cheer.   Who does not appreciate the open fireplaces at *The Lygon Arms* and *The George* at Buckden ?   Who has not stretched in comfort in the panelled room within the George at Odiham, or rested at the sign of the Bell, Barnby Moor (Fig. 102).   The inns are the birth-right of all travellers, with all the fitments, appurtenances, and the genialty that comes from contact with antiquity.   The old chairs, tables and sideboards for the time we are within the hospitable shelter are our personal property, at least, so we like to fancy, and to extend our coveting to the deep red bricks of garden walls, to the tiled barns, the stabling and the lofty proportions of assembly rooms.   Nothing in England can exercise a finer spell over the imagination than the lingering associations and customs of an inn.   Then it is that all we have read, heard or fancied of old English life reasserts its magic with the full flavour of what has been and to some extent, still is.   We have said that the inn rarely shows architectural perfection, rather it presents specimens of architecture.   There are, of course, such outstanding buildings of mediæval times as *The George* at Glastonbury (Fig. 60), and the perfection of seventeenth century craftsmanship is to be seen at Broadway, but in this work we are attempting to encompass the flavour of every type of inn, not excepting the later ones which continued to creep into the tradition before " Hotels " usurped their function.

Who cares a fig for the " Grand Babylon " when there is a poorer but more refined neighbour at hand ?   There is a tone about the old house that fits our thoughts and elevates our spirits—a seemly modesty derived from the ancestry of the race which the great hotel can never hope to gain, even expensively. We English, from our restlessness, have inherited the habit of making ourselves comfortable away from home. This explains why we are particularly observant of contrasts, and there is no surer means by which an enterprising landlord can secure the affections of his guests than by ministering to their eyes as well as to their bodily wants. Nothing encourages guests more than tidiness, and when this is combined with good taste and arrangement the trick is done. We have so far written of inns. There yet remains something to be said of those " hotels " built a century since which have so far escaped spoliation in the modern sense. We have recollections of the " Bedford " at Brighton, with its rare furniture of mahogany, and the bracket clock which announces the hours by playing " Tom Bowling." We have explored the rooms of *The Stamford Hotel* (Fig. 112) and *The King's Arms* at Christchurch (Fig. 116). We have admired the geometrical splendour of the staircase at *The Royal*, Devonport, the plan of Webb's at Liskeard, and that gem of Regency " houses," *The Royal* at Falmouth. Such " hotels " as the foregoing are newcomers in the lineage of inns ; they were succeeded by the huge caravanserai of the Victorian age which have railroad connections. England has many pleasant surprises for those who have an affection for her social intimacy, scenes that rise green to the memory above the passing of the years ; and not the least are the inns, recalling the foundations of home life and reviving the spirits of the despondent. It is astonishing how, in this country, respect for tradition lingers and will not be cheated. Not only do we enjoy the past in comfort and understand the felicity of chance company, but we can, if we so desire, actually experience some of the sensations of our ancestors. The ardent motorist, anxious for contrast and bent on genuine amusement, can, if he be so disposed, add to the enjoyment of his study of old inns by taking a ride on the top of a coach. There are some enthusiasts who have been carried in sedan chairs. There are coaches in various towns that are run by " whips " solely to perpetuate the old life of the road. We do not find the coaches crowded, for most people fight shy of the pleasure. To-day, no one ventures inside. We do not find luggage on the roof nor hampers of game depending from the rails. The turn-outs are resplendent, the team of bays or chestnuts the very pick of the stables. There is the guard in his livery who plays cheerful tunes and keeps careful guardianship over the passengers. The gentleman who acts as whip has a pride in the turn-out which would have delighted Tom Hennessy. The pace of the horses is a smart trot at ten good miles an hour, with all the fluency of motion that seems to communicate itself to the wheels and upwards through the springs to the outside passengers, as though pneumatic tyres had never been thought of. With what delight we watch the leaders taking an awkward corner, how we glance at the shop windows to see if the coach really represents a coloured engraving by Pollard, and how we welcome the smiling faces of shopkeepers who stand at the doors of their shops. There is an art in taking the salute just as there is in ignoring the modern folk who affect not to see the show. It is denied to the modern traveller by coach to drive into the arched entries of inns, or to experience the picture that at one time gave rise to feelings of pleased contentment as the journey progressed. We realise such things when travelling by car, and make a point of inspecting the kitchens, much to the surprise of many landlords of our acquaintance. And if we do not find hams and flitches of bacon suspended from the ceilings, there may be encountered many old cooking vessels and smoke jacks that have been resting for years. The subject is fascinating ; it calls for the fullest explanation, yet it can never be entirely accomplished within the pages of a single volume. Indeed, some inns almost demand a book to themselves.

As far as the introductory matter is concerned, we have endeavoured to compress more than five centuries of inn history within a single chapter, and having brought the account to the present day, we will proceed to analyse the inns and their accessories at greater length in the succeeding pages.

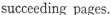

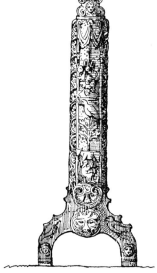

ANDIRON AT THE OLD COCK HOTEL, HALIFAX.   *L. A. Shuffrey, del.*

FIG. 54. A CYCLISTS' RENDEZVOUS: THE ANCHOR, RIPLEY, SURREY.
(Before alteration.)

FIG. 55. THE GEORGE, AMESBURY, WILTSHIRE.

Fig. 57. THE GEORGE, GLASTONBURY.

Fig. 56. THE CHEQUERS, TONBRIDGE.

THE WHITE HORSE, NEWARK
Hugh Mottram, A.R.I.B.A., del.

CHAPTER II

THE ENGLISH INN FROM THE FIFTEENTH CENTURY TO THE RESTORATION

In this chapter it is essential to speak of origins, but there is scant information of the wine shops and taverns of Roman Britain, or, for that matter, of Saxon and Norman times. It may be assumed that taverns of sorts were in existence both in town and country, but the nature of such places can best be judged by contemporary events. We have evidence of Saxon work in a few churches, but of the houses very little remains. It can be concluded, therefore, that the domestic architecture of Saxon times was in the main built in the form of framed timber structures filled in with wattle and daub or roughly wrought boarding. It can also be conjectured that the guest houses attached to the early monasteries were built of the same material.

London in Norman times had its vintners and its keepers of taverns, for visitors to the metropolis had to be accommodated. Little remains of Saxon domestic architecture, but there is an abundance of the stone

churches erected after the Conquest.   Despite the state of unrest in
which the country had been prior to and after the Conquest, there had
been trade of sorts, both internal and with the Continent, and this
implies inns and taverns for travellers and men-at-arms.

It should not be forgotten, also, that several large monasteries
had been established during the centuries preceding the Conquest, and
that the entertainment of travellers formed part of religious foundations.
There was also an apartment or apartments set aside for guests in the
great houses and castles.   In Saxon and Norman times the patriarchical
idea of the Common Hall was the centre for guests and the family, the
distinction between the company being the high seat for the family,
which was near the fire or brazier.   From this arrangement was
developed the College Hall, and the special dormitory and entertainment
chamber for travellers at the monastic establishment.   The furniture
consisted of rude benches and tables, the floor was strewn with rushes,
all weapons were left outside the door, and the entertainment was
conducted under the auspices of a monk, to whose charge the travellers
were by the rules of the order committed.   The times of meals varied
with the seasons.   There was breakfast about nine, the midday meal
at twelve and the evening meal at the close of daylight.   The guests
either slept on the floor or benches of the refectory or else retired to a
common dormitory.

Through the succeeding centuries down to the times of the dis-
solution of the monasteries somewhat similar customs prevailed.   There
were, however, many improvements, such as superior apartments for
guests of repute, the provision of washing-places and a *domicilium
necessarium*.   As the country began to benefit under Norman rule
so trade improved, and taverns and inns sprang up in London and the
cities.   There were three types of accommodation available in mediæval
times for travellers, namely, the castle, the monastery and the common
inn ;   we are thus confronted with social conditions dominated on all
sides by the extraordinary influence of the Church.

To foreigners who visit England the mediæval characteristics of
the cathedral cities and the country towns are most apparent, yet to
insular eyes such things are commonplace, and, save in certain circles,
pass almost without comment.   The churches are the most telling
monuments of Plantagenet and Tudor times, and provide a sure index
to the domestic architecture, which is rarer.   Let us take the example of
Coventry as it appears to-day.   The three churches indicate the mediæval
prosperity of the midland town, the timber-built houses, of which Ford's

Hospital is the most perfect example of its type, exist in sufficient numbers to enable a tolerable reconstruction of the city to be made. This is the more strange considering the modern development of Coventry. And so we could multiply our impressions of mediæval England. There is the rich field of East Anglia, the University centres of Oxford and Cambridge, the buildings of Glastonbury and Wells, of Chester and York, still existing as part of the fabric upon which the

FIG. 58.—THE FALCON YARD, CAMBRIDGE, 1875.

W. B. Redfarn, del.

social life of later times has been founded. There are, however, but few of the earliest inns and taverns in existence, for time and custom have conjointly laid no sparing hand on the places where travellers and guests were once sure of hospitality.

With inn signs there is a surer evidence of antiquity, especially to those learned in the decoration and origin of signs. But it is for the wise man to fight shy of those modern legends which assign a doubtful antiquity to certain inns whose skeletons have become obscured by the dressings of many ages. *The Mitre* at Oxford is beyond question an ancient house, for the vaulted cellars below the pavement belong to Plantagenet days. *The Angel* at Grantham (Figs. 1, 13 and 14) is more precious than the famous *George* at Glastonbury (Fig. 60), for its stone-built walls and entrance gateway, standing full to the street, have an assurance of ancestry that is disturbing even to the timber-built inns of Tudor days. There are remains of mediæval inns at Southampton, at Aylesbury (Fig. 72), Exeter and Salisbury, but such are fragmentary, and the more precious by reason of the features of structure that are still in evidence.

Of the mediæval inns of Southwark nothing remains, for nearly all suffered destruction by fire in the seventeenth century. For want of more precise evidence, it can be assumed for the purpose of a general survey of the subject that the inn of Plantagenet times, whether stone- or timber-built, had a street frontage with a central archway which gave access to a courtyard, as in Fig. 61. Round the inn yard were grouped the galleries on to which the sleeping apartments opened. Behind the first courtyard was another with stabling and storehouses. The size of the yards varied with the importance of the inn. The inn had become a feature of social life in the fifteenth century. It then functioned as a species of general office where men could foregather and transact business; it was a place of entertainment, not only for food and drink, but providing the settings for the plays and mummings which, sanctioned by the Church, were enacted in the principal courtyard, the stage being a waggon requisitioned for the purpose.

A concise account of the fourteenth century inn is not possible, but there is the lease and inventory of the Tabard for reference, which gives some idea of the house much as it was in Chaucer's time. We must not lose sight of the fact that fragments of old inns of Plantagenet date exist in the fabric of inns which outwardly express the fashion of later times. Thus to know the inns of a particular period it becomes essential to be able to trace the evolution of the inn through the ages. The individual inns, therefore, provide a truer narrative than it is possible to include within the pages of a book. The church influenced and overshadowed most things, there were even church houses or inns, such as the Church House at Holne, on Dartmoor, which were run by the church for the accommodation of travellers. It was no accident that caused Chaucer to include twelve ecclesiastics in his account of the Canterbury Pilgrims, there were the gentle Prioress, the nun and three priests, the Limitour licensed by the Bishop to hear confessions, the Oxford Clerk, the Monk of Rabelaisian mould, the Town Parson, the Soumpner— or Summoner—and the hypocritical Pardoner with his stock of sham holy relics. What a sight for the rabble, for men-at-arms, carriers, farmers and friends, was afforded at the inns of country towns in the time of Chaucer ! The King and his court travelled from castle to castle, only making occasional use of the Maison du Roi ; the great nobles travelled from manor to manor at different seasons carrying tapestries and the more precious of their household goods with them.

The frequenters of the Plantagenet inns are therefore reduced to merchants, a few ecclesiastics, soldiers and men-at-arms, and to the local customers attracted to the centre of social intercourse. The inns provided accommodation for judges on circuit for trials and inquests, and they became by a natural process local exchanges for country districts. Shakespeare makes constant reference to the inns of the fifteenth century ; he drew on the inns and inn life of his own time for details and incidents, some of which will be referred to. Many inns claim to date from the fourteenth century, this hypothesis being based on the presence of some structural beams of unusual size. That an inn may have been established on the site at this early date is beyond dispute, but it is rare to find authentic fragments. There are vaulted cellars beneath some of the houses in St. Albans, which may have been the vaults of ancient hostelries, and almost every city in England holds some antiquities of the kind ; but the authentic inn of the fourteenth century is rare, and the stone front of *The Angel* at Grantham (Fig. 13) is the more valuable on that account.

The inn of the late fifteenth and sixteenth centuries happily still exists in every part of the country. There are such classic examples as *The Bell* at Thetford, *The King's Head* at Aylesbury (Fig. 72), *The Star* at Alfriston (Fig. 65), the inns of Tewkesbury (Figs. 69 and 266), and of Chester (Figs. 91 and 273). We can, however, turn to a country inn, *The George* at Norton St. Philip (Fig. 66), on the borders of Somerset and Wilts, which possesses some features of the early fifteenth century. This fine house has been variously described as an hostelry and a place wherein the wool market was held.

At one time the whole of the manor of Norton St. Philip, including *The George Inn*, belonged to the Carthusian Priory of Hinton, and this seems explanatory of the fact that the inn served as a market, for in the time of Edward I, both the weekly market and the annual wool fair were held by the Priory. In those days the large upper room was

used by the traders in wool, which formed the chief industry of Norton
St. Philip, and the other part of the house was an hostelry.   When
first built, early in the fifteenth century, the whole structure was of
stone.   The projecting half timber storeys which divide the front
horizontally into three divisions are of later date as the stone quoins
at the gable end show.   The alteration points to the destruction by
fire of the upper part of the inn in the late fifteenth or early sixteenth
century, when opportunity was taken to patch and alter the ancient
house to its present form.   The earlier stone porch and the bay windows
are practically as first built.   The view from the back exhibits features
which are unusually picturesque.   For example the octagonal stone-
roofed turret stairway and a fragment of the ancient gallery point to
the dependencies of the original fabric.   At the back the original stone
work and traceried windows remain as first built.

It is for the most part a genuine survival of an early inn ; the individual stones are as eloquent of the social life of the middle ages as any
chronicler could wish.   This house has taken to itself the impressions
of five centuries as though the very materials of which it is composed
were sensitive of their purpose.   Nothing else can explain the articu-
lation of the front, the accidental grouping of the windows, or the very
human foibles exhibited by the patchings and additions.   To this inn
Cromwell came with a party of his Roundheads, and not many years
after, the life of the handsome Monmouth was attempted while he was
standing at one of the windows.

The Pilgrim's Inn at Glastonbury (Fig. 60), which was built between
the years 1470-1475 by Abbot John de Selwood, for accommodating
pilgrims and others visiting the abbey, speaks of the time when the
Church still exercised the dominant influence on social life.   The inn,
now called *The George Hotel*, faces south.   The freestone of which
it is built has stood the test of time and weather unimpaired.   The
front is only 34 feet in width, but the building looks twice that dimension.
The original designer knew his business well, for he contrived to embody
in one design, without any sense of overcrowding, the dissimilar
features of a three-storied bay, an archway, also a projecting support
for the sign, and buttresses.   There resulted one of the finest examples
of a panelled design, which at this period was a distinctive feature for
town buildings in the western region.   The majority of the compart-
ments are pierced and glazed, the remainder not required for windows
being filled in with solid masonry.   Interest attaches to the three
carved panels over the arched entry ; two show the armorial bearings

of the Abbey and Edward IV. respectively, while the third shows a
shield without trace of arms. At the side of the doorway is the stone

FIG. 59.—COURTYARD OF THE MERMAID, RYE

F. J. Watson Hart, del.

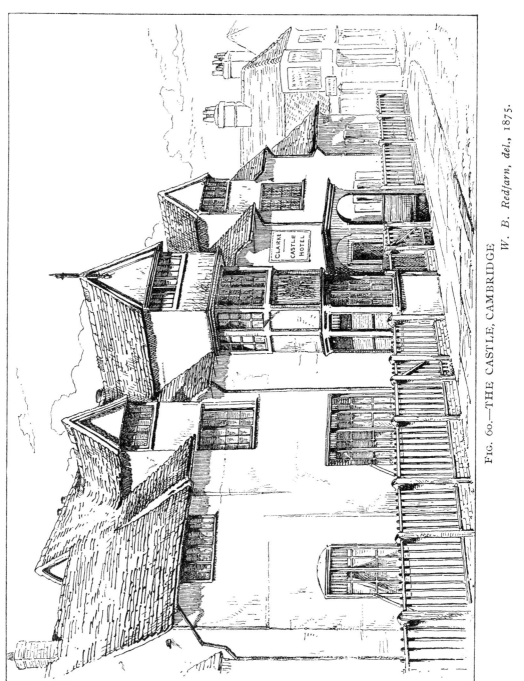

FIG. 60.—THE CASTLE, CAMBRIDGE.

W. B. Redfarn, del., 1875.

Fig. 61. THE NEW INN, GLOUCESTER, A CENTURY AGO. (John Britton del.)

FIG. 62. THE BELL, WALTHAM St. LAWRENCE, BERKSHIRE.

FIG. 63. THE FIGHTING COCKS, ST. ALBANS, HERTFORDSHIRE.

FIG. 64. THE DOLPHIN, FORMERLY BISHOP HALL'S PALACE, HEIGHAM,
NORWICH. (Dated 1587, 1595, and 1615.)

FIG 65. THE STAR, ALFRISTON, SUSSEX.

Fig. 66. THE GEORGE, NORTON ST. PHILIP, SOMERSET.

FIG. 67. THE BARLEY MOW, CLIFTON HAMPDEN, OXON.

FIG. 68. THE FOUR SWANS, WALTHAM, ESSEX.

FIG. 69. THE BELL, TEWKESBURY.

Fig. 71. FORMERLY AN INN, SAFFRON WALDEN, ESSEX.

Fig. 70. IN THE COURTYARD, THE OSTRICH, COLNBROOK, MIDDLESEX. (v. also Fig. 73).

Fig. 72. THE XVth CENTURY WINDOW OF THE KING'S HEAD, AYLESBURY.

Fig. 73. THE OSTRICH, COLNBROOK. (*v. also* Fig. 70.)

FIG. 74. THE QUEEN'S HEAD, ISLINGTON. (T. Hosmer Shepherd del.)

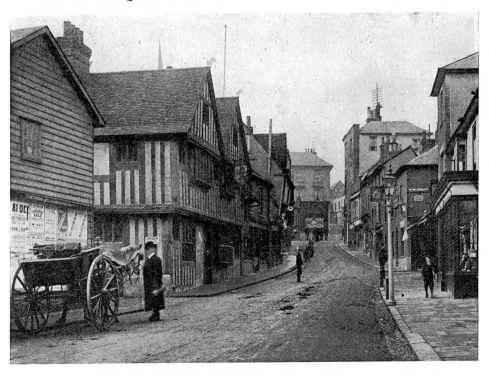

FIG 75. BRIDGE STREET, BISHOP'S STORTFORD. (*v. also* Fig. 253.)

FIG. 76. FIREPLACE IN THE BULL, OTFORD.

FIG. 77. FIREPLACE IN THE WHITE HORSE, SHERE.

Fig. 79.　THE LUGGER, FOWEY, CORNWALL.

Fig. 78.　PANELLED ROOM FORMERLY AT THE
REINDEER, BANBURY.

Fig. 80. Front view.

Fig. 81. Back view. (*v. also Figs.* 94 *and* 189.)

THE WHITE HART SCOLE, NORFOLK. (1655.)

FIG. 82.   THE JOLLY SAILOR, WEST LOOE, CORNWALL.

FIG. 83.   A BIT OF XVIITH CENTURY SOUTHWARK.   (Wenceslaus Hollar del.)

Fig. 84. THE BELL, STILTON, HUNTINGDONSHIRE.

Fig. 85. THE LYGON ARMS, BROADWAY, WORCESTERSHIRE.

FIG. 86. THE POMFRET ARMS, FORMERLY THE SARACEN'S HEAD, TOWCESTER, NORTHANTS.

FIG. 87. THE GREYHOUND, CORFE, DORSET.

Fig. 88. THE WHITE HART, PENKRIDGE,
STAFFORDSHIRE.

Fig. 89. THE FEATHERS, LUDLOW. (*v. also*
Figs. 92, 93, *and* 96.)

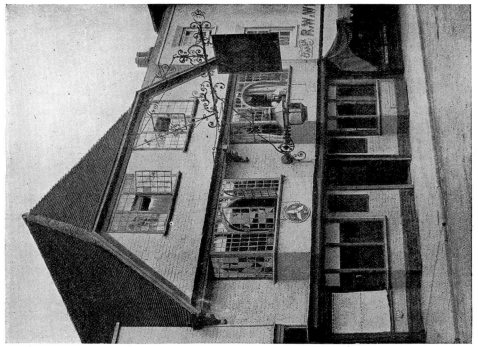

Fig. 91. THE FALSTAFF, CANTERBURY.

Fig. 90. THE BEAR AND BILLET, CHESTER.

FIG. 92.   The Dining Room.

Photos by W. Harper, Ludlow.

FIG. 93.   The Coffee Room.

INTERIORS OF THE FEATHERS, LUDLOW.

column and pier which carries the shaped bracket supporting the sign, originally St. George and the Dragon, which was sculptured and blazoned in colours. The little shields in the cornices have crosses, and the initials of the builder, " I. S." interwoven, occur on one side. From between the battlements of the bay window, a sculptured figure looks out holding a cup. It is the sole survivor of several, testifying to the mediæval love of a jest at the expense of the topers within. It is a rich house to look upon, and there can be little doubt of the fact that at one time the internal fitments, of which no trace exists, were of the same rich character as the front.

Another inn of Tudor times is *The King's Head* at Aylesbury, a timber-framed structure, exhibiting in its great window (Fig. 72), as in the moulded ribs of its external and internal framings, that disregard for time, labour and material which was the creed of mediæval builders. The timber houses of French Row, St. Albans, part of *The White Hart* on Holywell Hill, St. Albans, and a still older inn near by prove the inns of cathedral cities and abbey towns to have been buildings of the first rank. In York the more ancient inns have been destroyed, but the houses forming the Shambles, with their huge projections and nodding gables, no less than the massive timberings, enable us to reconstruct the scenery which made up town life in the Middle Ages.

The old *Fighting Cocks Inn* at St. Albans (Fig. 63) has an antiquity assigned to it which is doubtful. The present octagonal building of timber may or may not be older than the late fourteenth century. Its situation suggests that it may have formed originally a species of fishing lodge for the benefit of the monks, but its situation near the mill, the River Ver and the ancient causeway, accounts for its longevity as a place of entertainment. The sign was painted a few years since by Mr. William Webster Hoare, an amateur artist, who in his youth had been friendly with the famous Joe Nash.

Another interesting inn of the late fourteenth century is *The Cooper's Arms* in Tilehouse Street, Hitchin, the three traceried windows forming the whole expanse of the ground floor storey being all that remain externally of the original structure The entry to *The Angel* at Guildford and portions of the buildings in the courtyard can also be assigned to the early Tudor period. And so we come to take interest in other Tudor relics, such as the older parts of *The George* at Stamford (Figs. 103 and 104), *The Lion Inn* at Wingham, Kent, with its corner post and spur piece, the twin gables of *The King Charles* at Poole and the highly ornate timbered front of *The Bell* at Tewkesbury (Fig. 69). Of the smaller inns of Early Tudor times, *The Barley Mow* at Clifton Hampden, near Wallingford Bridge on the Thames (Fig. 67), has the interest of showing its structural timber rising in whalebone fashion from the ground to the underside of the hooded gable, an interesting survival of a very early form of construction before the practice of projecting one storey in advance of another was reverted to.

East Anglia is particularly rich in Tudor inns. There is *The Rose and Crown* at Sudbury, the house originally an inn called *The Black Horse*, where Gainsborough was born, and *The Castle* at Long Melford, originally a clothing town of importance ; there is *The Bull*, at Sudbury in Suffolk, which had a galleried passage at the back. There are the Tudor framings to the inn entries in the main street at Buntingford.

In Colchester there is *The Red Lion*, originally *The St. George and Dragon*, and many timbered houses with corner posts, which in other times were inns. Ipswich has many relics of the period, most of the ancient inns having carved corner posts. At the sign of *The Half Moon* is the oft-repeated mediæval joke of a fox in meek and demure mien with hood and cowl and with arms folded preaching to geese. *The Four Swans* at Waltham Cross (Fig. 68) claims to date from the fourteenth century, but there is little above ground to support the claim.

The White Horse at Newark until recent years could show some signs of its earlier structure, the gallery to the courtyard over the entry being its chief feature (p. 45). Another ancient inn is *The Saracen's Head*, Southwell. There is the inn at Fotheringay and the remains of the stone-built *George Inn* at Bedford (Fig. 19). *The Swan* at Elstow (Fig. 238) has the timbering and herringbone brickwork of the late Tudor period, while *The Lion* at Buckden can show internal timbering coeval in date with the building of the Bishop of Lincoln's palace near by. Portions of *The George* at Huntingdon date from Tudor times, and the narrow yard of *The Golden Lion* at St. Ives recalled the longevity of the Tudor hostelry.

There are many timbered or plastered houses at Saffron Walden (Fig. 71) which in the fifteenth century may well have been taverns, and this distinction is shared by some of the houses at Bishop's Stortford (Figs. 75 and 253). The back of *The Luttrell Arms* at Dunster, although of later date, shows the survival of earlier traditions in stone building, with a window of carved timber.

In the days of Elizabeth the prosperity of the realm was again in the ascendant. London and other cities were beginning to affect

FIG. 95. THE ENTRANCE, THE LYGON ARMS, BROADWAY.
(v. also Fig. 85.)

FIG. 94. THE STAIRCASE, THE WHITE HART, SCOLE,
NORFOLK. (1655.) (v. also Figs. 80, 81, and 189.)

Fig. 97. THE GEORGE, SALISBURY.

Fig. 96. DETAIL OF THE FEATHERS, LUDLOW.
(*v. Fig.* 89.)

new fashions in buildings as in dress ; intercourse between towns was growing more common ; but the dominant influence of the Church had long since vanished, and in place of the guest houses of the monasteries new inns had been built for travellers. The suppression of the monasteries altered the whole social outlook of the country, and threw the poorer class of travellers on to the charity of the parish in which they found themselves.   Then were the orders for the apprehension of vagrants made stringent.   Then did the tramp, the courtesyman and the highway robber increase in number.

The London tavern of the third quarter of the sixteenth century, and likewise the hostelry, had gained a fuller significance. Stage waggons for the transport of goods were coming into favour, but the pack horse train and carriers still looked after the transport of smaller merchandise. In the first part of *King Henry IV.*, Shakespeare, in Scene 4, describes a scene in a room at the Boar's Head Tavern, Cheapside, and again, in the second part of *Henry IV.*, Scene 4, the poet refers to the same house.   Previously, in Act ii., is described an inn yard at Rochester, which, although it refers to the year 1402, has evidently been drawn by the poet from life.

ROCHESTER—An Inn Yard.

Enter a Carrier, with a Lanthorn in his hand.

First Carrier : Heigh ho !   An't be not four by the day, I'll be hanged : Charles' wain is over the new chimney, and yet our horse not packed.   What, ostler !

Ostler (within) : Anon, anon.

First Carrier : I prithee, Tom, beat Cut's saddle, put a few flocks in the point ; the poor jade is wrung in the withers out of all cess.

Enter another Carrier.

Second Carrier : I think this be the most villainous house in all London Road for fleas : I am stung like a tench.

First Carrier : Like a tench ?   By the mass, there is ne'er a king in Christendom could be better bit than I have been since the first cock.

Second Carrier : Why, they will allow us ne'er a jorden, and then we leak in the chimney ; and your chamberlie breeds fleas like a loach.

First Carrier : What, ostler ! Come away and be hanged, come away !

Second Carrier : I have a gammon of bacon and two razes of ginger, to be delivered as far as Charing Cross.

First Carrier : 'Odsbody! The turkeys in my pannier are quite starved. What, ostler! A plague on thee! Hast thou never an eye in thy head? Can'st not hear? An 'twere not as good a deed as drink, to break the pate of thee, I am a very villian. Come, and be hanged! Hast no faith in thee?

Enter Gadshill.

Gadshill : Sirrah carrier, what time do you mean to come to London?

Second Carrier : Time enough to go to bed with a candle, I warrant thee. Come, neighbour Mugs, we'll call up the gentlemen : they will along with company, for they have great charge.

[Exeunt Carriers.

To the national poet we are indebted for the scene in the induction to the *Taming of the Shrew*, which describes an alehouse of the late sixteenth century.

INDUCTION.

SCENE I.—BEFORE AN ALEHOUSE ON A HEATH.

Enter Hostess and Sly.

Sly : I'll pheeze you, in faith!

Hostess : A pair of stocks, you rogue!

Sly : Y'are a baggage : the Slys are no rogues : look in the chronicles ; we came in with Richard Conqueror, therefore, *paucas pallabris* ; let the world slide : *Sessa!*

Hostess : You will not pay for the glasses you have burst?

Sly : No, not a denier. Go by, Jeronimy, go to thy cold bed, and warm thee.

Hostess : I know my remedy, I must go fetch the third-borough.

Sly : Third, or fourth, or fifth borough, I'll answer him by law. I'll not budge an inch, boy ; let him come, and kindly.
(*Lies down on the ground and falls asleep.*)

The Elizabethan inn and tavern is still to be seen in the country town. At Ampthill there is the interesting entry to the yard near *The King's Head,* which at one time formed part of the collection of inns of this little-known market town of mid-Bedfordshire. From this yard the stage waggon and the carrier started for Bedford and London. There are the timber-fronted inns named *The Bell* at Woodbridge, *The Old Reindeer* at Banbury (Fig. 78)—alas! sadly restored— many of the smaller hostelries of Cambridge, at Newport, Essex, and Bury St. Edmund's. Plymouth could formerly show such inns and taverns as *The Old Four Castles, The Rose and Crown, The Turk's Head Inn* and *The White Hart*, and the inns of Elizabethan London were legion. At Fowey there is *The Old Lugger Inn* (Fig. 79), and the quays of Bristol City at one time were renowned for the gabled taverns which were the haven of seafaring men and voyagers. Shakespeare describes a scene at the Garter in the *Merry Wives of Windsor*. We have, too, in *The Ostrich* at Colnbrook (Figs. 70 and 73) one of the most representative of country town inns of the sixteenth century.

The Dolphin at Norwich, formerly the Bishop's Palace (Fig. 64), bears the date of 1615, though parts are of earlier date, and is chiefly interesting by reason of its Tudor detail, which has survived into the seventeenth century. On the other hand, the inn at Scole (Figs. 80, 81, 94 and 189) is perhaps the most perfect example now standing of an inn of the mid-seventeenth century. And so we could go on enumerating inn after inn of the amazing and adventurous epoch when so much was done to increase the national prosperity. The early years of the seventeenth century witnessed no great change from the preceding age. The inns of London and Southwark became busier in the reigns of James I and Charles I. Drinking taverns were added to the number of older establishments in London. There were 7,000 tobacco shops in London alone, and the custom of going out to Kentish Town, Highgate and Islington to drink and make merry, as described by Ben Jonson, was beginning to form part of a Londoner's recreation.

In the early seventeenth century the inns on the main highways began to be improved. Such houses as *The Bell* at Stilton (Fig. 84), a fine stone-built structure, in which can be traced the influence of the Cotswold tradition, came to be built. To this period can be assigned *The Lygon Arms* at Broadway (Figs. 85 and 95), the remodelling of *The Mitre* at Oxford, the building of the White Horse at Dorking, the George at Amesbury (Fig. 55), and the Chandos Arms at Edgware (p. 61). Then were built the old inns at Amersham, Missenden and Wendover, the Falstaff at Canterbury (Fig. 91), the older part of *The George* at Stamford (Figs. 103 and 104), the inns at Baldock, *The King's Arms* at Weldon Magna, Northamptonshire, and *The Talbot* at Oundle (Fig. 24). There is an old house at Markyate Street, once an inn, which by reason of its Jacobean front deserves mention. There is a house, now a farmhouse, at Little Brickhill, on Watling Street, and *The White Horse* at Hockcliffe (p. 70), with its strange assortment of carving from the Manor House at Toddington, built by John Thorpe. All the latter were known at a later date to Daniel Defoe.

Finally we come to the period of the Restoration, when tavern life was revived after the country had experienced the regime of the Commonwealth. Reference has already been made to that most stately inn of the later seventeenth century, *The Haycock* at Wansford (Figs. 20-23), a stone-built house of great size, perfect in every detail. This inn was built at the time Pepys made his journeys to Brampton; it is now the country seat of Sir Beche Cunard. The *Sea Horse* at Deene is another Northamptonshire house which, with the Haycock, shares the distinction of inheriting some Cotswold features as far north as the River Nene. *The Pomfret Arms* at Towcester, formerly *The Saracen's Head* (Fig. 86), and as such described by Charles Dickens, is a house of the late seventeenth century. Then we have *The Greyhound* at Corfe (Fig. 87), *The Judge's Lodgings*, formerly part of *The Antelope*, at Dorchester, and the inn at Chagford, on Dartmoor. A goodly company of Restoration inns.

FIG. 98.—YARD OF THE GEORGE, NORTON ST. PHILIP (*v.* FIG. 66)

Hugh Mottram, A.R.I.B.A., del.

We are now arrived at the days enlivened by the writings of Cotton and Izaak Walton, times made familiar to us by the diary of Samuel

FIG. 99.　THE CROSS KEYS, ST. NEOTS, HUNTINGDONSHIRE.

FIG. 100.　THE DINING-ROOM, THE DUKE'S HEAD, KING'S LYNN.

FIG. 101. FISH INN, BROADWAY, WORCESTERSHIRE.

FIG. 102. THE BELL, BARNBY MOOR, YORKSHIRE.

Pepys, with his notes on the inns he frequented in London and the country. Stage coaches were beginning to be established, and road books written describing the main and cross routes from London. Travelling had become more usual for every class. London had become the great port for the reception and transmission of all the goods in the whole of the country, and new docks for the East India trade had been established. The clothmakers of the West Country, the ironfounders of Sussex, the colliers of the North and the tin miners of Cornwall were producing on a scale hitherto unknown. London a few years later was in the hands of the builders. It was a time for drinking and carousing. Pepys is constantly getting " foxed " with drink. The sports of bull and bear baiting were still carried on, theatres were established under royal patronage and the whole social fabric was undergoing a subtle change from the mediævalism which had pertained down through the centuries to the Protectorate.

The favourite places of resort in the City were the galleries of the Royal Exchange, the Piazza at Covent Garden, while Spring Gardens and Vauxhall were also favouite places of resort outside the City. In London, coffee-houses were set up to compete with the taverns, and to these places of resort can be attributed the development of the London Club at a later period.

THE CHANDOS ARMS, EDGWARE

Hugh Mottram, A.R.I.B.A., del.

CHAPTER III

THE DEVELOPMENT OF THE HOSTELRY IN THE LATE SEVENTEENTH, EIGHTEENTH AND EARLY NINETEENTH CENTURIES

THE story of the Inns of London is told in another chapter, but it is to London, again, we must turn to investigate the changes of custom and travel which, spreading outwards from the capital, left an indelible impress on the buildings along the main roads, such as those under discussion. The Restoration, big event as it was, would not have singled out the reign of Charles the Second as being anything exceptional but for the dual disasters of the Plague and the Fire. From the diaries of Pepys and Evelyn, as well as the imaginative account of the Plague written some years later by Daniel Defoe, we gather impressions of the attitude and the sufferings of the populace. Writing in September, 1665, when the pestilence was at its height, Pepys says, " To the Tower, and then sent for the weekly Bill, and find 8,252 dead in all, and of these 6,978 of the plague, which is a most dreadful number and shows reason to fear that the plague had got that hold that it will yet continue among us. Thence to Brentford, reading ' The Villaine,' a pretty good play, all the way. There a coach of Mr. Povy's stood ready for me, and he at his house ready to come in, and so we together merrily to Swakely to Sir R. Viner."

It was at this time that all who could began to depart from London. The roads teemed with carts and waggons. The Court left town and the legal business of the country was transferred to Oxford. The Plague caused the suspension of all business, to the great benefit of the Dutch. London, which after the return of the King had again begun to prosper, as befitted a seaport, was suddenly disturbed by the stoppage of of its industries, and soon after the whole trade of the country was affected. The roads, save for the passing of fugitives, carried little or no traffic. The woollen industry in the Devonshire towns was affected. The ironworkers of Sussex, the tin mines of Cornwall, and workers in other branches of industry, felt the full effect of the disaster which had come upon the Capital. A year later, early in the morning of Sunday, the second of September, the Great Fire broke out at the house of a baker in Pudding Lane, Thames Street. At night Pepys stood watching the fire from Bankside. On the following Wednesday he trod on the smouldering embers of the once proud mediæval city.

The city had suffered both pestilence and fire, the people had been tried and in most cases had lost their all, but the national spirit was undaunted. In the short space of four years a newer London was in being with many thousand fair houses of brick, with new halls for the City Companies and some new churches. And so through the succeeding years, thanks to the genius of Sir Christopher Wren and his school, the untiring industry of the craftsmen as well as the enterprise of the building owners, a new order of things was created. Prior to this London and the majority of English towns were mediæval in character. There had been, it is true, departures from the national tradition earlier in the century, but these by comparison with the rebuilding of the city of London were insignificant. It is therefore to the years that succeeded the Plague and the Fire that must be assigned the exact time when the compromise between the mediæval and the modern took place. We have, therefore, at our disposal in the architecture of this time a complete index to the social fabric of the late seventeenth century, and we are enabled to understand the subsequent developments in the eighteenth century. Trade began to revive, and a newer order of merchants arose in the City. The call of London began to reassert itself. The roads again became frequented, and as a result many new inns were built in the country towns and old ones were refronted to accord with the newer idea of brick building, but it can be seen that regional traits persisted and builders and artificers adapted the new fashion to local materials. *The Haycock* at Wansford, already described, one of the largest inns on the Great North Road (Figs. 20—22), can be considered to be one of the first of the hostelries of the time.   There is *The Saracen's Head* at Towcester, now *The Pomfret Arms*, previously mentioned (Fig. 86), a stone-built house, with heavy sashed windows of a later date. This is the inn immortalised in " Pickwick Papers " as the meeting place of Slurk and Pott.   In Stamford Town the older part of the Stamford Hotel is eloquent of the revival of York and London traffic in the late seventeenth century. *The Salutation Inn* at Topsham, Devon, belongs to the opening years of the eighteenth century ; it was much frequented by Dutch dealers.   *The Black Lion*, St. Michaels, St. Albans, is another interesting house of this period.   There are old inns at Amersham, such as the back portion of *The Griffin*, which, with the older part of *The George* at Pangbourne, and *The George* at Buckden (Figs. 52, 53), belong to the Stuart age, but like many of the seventeenth century inns have since been refronted.

The eighteenth century in its opening years brought further changes in the building of inns and hostelries in every part of the country.   In the reigns of the first and second Georges the full influence of London began to be reflected in the country towns all along the roads.   *The Duke's Head* at King's Lynn (Fig. 100), which Bell, the architect, built as a mansion, about this time became an inn, and on this account comes within the category of Stuart inns, and in like manner the inns of Southwark (Fig. 2) which were rebuilt after the minor fires in the Borough are to be classed as seventeenth century houses (see Figs. 138, 139, 140, 141, 143).   One of the best inns of the period of George the First is *The Sun* at Hitchin, which has a three-storied front to Sun Street, with a large entry to the courtyard.   *The George* at Buckden (Figs. 52, 53) is a house that has obviously grown by successive stages to suit increasing traffic.   Its archway is low, suggesting that in 1730 the coaches that lumbered between London and York carried no passengers outside.   The brick front is of the straight waistcoated early Georgian type with a deep flat parapet above the third range of windows. The George occupies a goodly length of the village street, and part of it has been let off.   At the side are to be seen the rooms used by generations of post boys, the old settles, fireplaces and adjoining stables marking the scene of former activity when the call came to ride north and south post haste.   There is the brick front of *The George* at Axminster, also a three-storied house with a vista through the gateway to the irregular courtyard. These inns are usually the most important-looking examples of architecture in the street scenery of country towns. *The George* at Pangbourne, previously mentioned, shows a three-storied façade of which the upper windows are panels painted to resemble windows. In this case it is as though a former proprietor had become ashamed of the Stuart building and wished to present a bolder face to his cramped attics. *The Crosskeys* at St. Neots (Fig. 99) underwent transformation about the year 1730, when the front was newly bricked and the bay windows were added, and the same remarks apply to the pretentious front of the White Hart at Ampthill in Bedfordshire. Nearer London we have the three-storied front of *The White Hart* in High Street, Southall. There is *The Lion* at Hartford Bridge and *The White Hart* at Hook, fine houses of early Georgian character. There are ornate fronts at St. Neots in Huntingdonshire which, built originally as inns, have now succumbed to the exigencies of modern commerce. Fenny Stratford on the Watling Street could once show many inns, but to-day only the antiquary can trace them. There remain however *The Cock* and *The Bull*, two noted coaching inns famous for the tales and rumours which are said to have emanated from those who frequented them in the eighteenth century, which gave rise to the expression " a Cock and Bull story." Dr. Johnson knew *The Swan* at Lichfield, which has come down to us practically unaltered from the time when the great man was a schoolboy. An inn of large size dating from the middle of the eighteenth century is *The Rutland Arms* at Newmarket, which is a classic essay in brick with a pedimented feature over the entry from the courtyard. *The Sun* at Tewkesbury dates from about 1745. *The Old George* at Aylesbury, now the headquarters of a territorial regiment, dates from the 1770 period. At this house, until a few years since, most of the old plate was in service, but lack of custom was the cause of its closing before motoring gave new life to the roads. In the third quarter of the eighteenth century *The Bell* at Barnby Moor (Fig. 102) came into its position as a first-class inn. About the year 1740 additions were made to *The George* at Stamford, and it was at this time that the northern wing to the courtyard with the twin bow windows was added (Fig. 104). *The White Hart* at Launceston is a modest three-storied house of the second half of the eighteenth century, crowned in true west country fashion with a slate roof of low pitch. At Grantham are to be seen two remarkable examples of the third quarter of the eighteenth century which are respectively *The George* (Fig. 31) and the additions to *The Angel* (Fig. 105). The George is an outstanding instance of the architectural taste of the day.   It is a three-storied house of brick with two pavilion features which terminate the grouping of five windows.   At the centre there is a rusticated entry with the date 1789 on the key stone, but recent alterations have deprived this inn of the character it possessed when Nicholas Nickelby stopped outside on the memorable journey to Dotheboys Hall.   The additions to *The Angel* at Grantham appear like a set of chambers from the Middle Temple : the fronts to the courtyard no less than the extensive range of stabling presenting that trim uniformity characteristic of late eighteenth century taste.   The shaping of the arches over the windows recalls the cock affected by the military for hats, a fashion inspired from France. These sets of rooms are planned independently of the mediæval portion of the house, but a passage lit by a Palladian window serves the purpose of a bricky ligament over the arched entry.   One of the most perfect Georgian inns is *The White Lion* at Cobham in Surrey.   This house has the gentlemanly look of being the rendezvous if not of the " nobility " at least of the " gentry."   Jane Austen refers to the Dolphin at Southampton, and so does Fanny Burney.   It is moreover a favourite with Mr. Belloc.

In general, the majority of inns in country towns which were built in the eighteenth century, as well as those of earlier date which assumed the scarlet coat of brick or the grey surtout of stone in response to the mode, have a family resemblance in so far as the doors and windows are concerned.   The inn, however, can never be confused with the houses of the same date.   The Georgian builders understood their work and continued to erect buildings suited to the main purpose of providing accommodation for travellers, which at this stage in the history of road travel was developing in an unprecedented way.   Custom had decreed the arrangement of an inn plan.   There was the usual courtyard with its arched or beamed entry.   There was a hall for receiving guests, a main staircase, a coffee room and a dining parlour.   Some inns could boast a special apartment for dining coach passengers only.   In addition there were smaller apartments known respectively by the names Sun, Moon, Star, Crescent or Paragon.   From 1700 to the year 1760 the arched entries were low, for until the latter date outside passengers were not encouraged.   After the accession of George the Third, when outside travelling became more general, the inside passengers were treated as belonging to an inferior order.   Not only did landlords show increased respect to the outside passengers, but a subtle compliment was paid to the coach proprietors by the landlords when alterations to the arched entries

were made to their respective inns. As we write so the pleasant fronts
of the eighteenth century inns rise to our minds—what important places
they were to our ancestors and how conspicuous they appear to-day
amidst the picturesque setting of the streets of the towns and villages
of England. There is *The Bull* at Royston (Fig. 108) known to generations of Cambridge undergraduates in the eighteenth and early nineteenth
centuries and now awaiting rediscovery. The front is plain enough,
the elevation to the courtyard is slightly more interesting, but the bow
window to the kitchen redeems the house from the reproach of being
too severe. This bow is unique among bows. Externally it is of the
sashed window type, having three lights to each of its storeys, but
within there exists an example of a neat and convenient filment, which
must have delighted the thrifty ladies who, travelling as inside passengers,
sometimes took their meals in the kitchen. For it became the custom
for certain customers of " inferior rank " to be shown to the kitchen.
The Sugar Loaf at Dunstable is another, but a larger, example of early
Georgian design. With *The Bull* at Redbourn (Fig. 107) this house
shared the honour of being a stopping place for passengers by the
heavy coaches to the north-west which were horsed by Sherman. *The
Rose and Crown* at Saffron Walden is yet another house with a Georgian
front. This inn was remodelled in 1874 by Eden Nesfield, and in this
regard it is an example of successful work by an architect who understood
the character of his subject. Many of the Georgian inns have nothing
externally to recommend them except their homely aspect and the
simple dignity of a row of sashed windows. Such is the case of Goldings
Hotel at Callington in Cornwall. But we respect the reticence that
prompted the well-intentioned designers to a plain rendering, for they
knew how to proportion windows and could add a portico or shape
an archway with the best architects out of London. Sometimes
architects of no mean talent were employed, as was the case for *The
Red Lion* at Hatfield (Fig. 109), which, standing just outside the town
and near to the house of the Cecils, took on the important air which
has never deserted it. Until quite recently this house could show an
extensive range of timber stabling, forming an appendage to its trim
brickwork and contrasting with the Chinese Gothic of the portico. *The
Swan Hotel* at Bedford (Fig. 117) is perhaps the most correct of late
eighteenth century inns. This house was built in 1794 from designs
furnished in all probability by Henry Holland, and in it the architect
incorporated the late seventeenth century staircase from the dismantled
mansion at Houghton Conquest. The Swan can show refinement of

architectural taste which belongs to the mansion, yet it functioned in
the late eighteenth century as a public inn.

Another house which has classical pretentions is *The White Hart*
at Salisbury. This inn was entirely rebuilt at the close of the eighteenth
century. It is a three-storied affair with a portico feature at the centre
highly Ionic in mien. The windows have lost their sash bars, but the effigy
of a White Hart still surmounts the royal arms in the tympanum of the
pediment, and the great lamps on either side of the lower porch suggest
a species of memorial to the myriad lamps of wheeled vehicles which long
since passed off the road.

A coach passenger arriving at any of these inns a hundred and
twenty-five years ago would have expected to find the highest degree
of comfort and elegance. If the coach was timed to stop for half an hour
to enable the passenger to dine, he would find the waiters in readiness
to assist him with his hat, shawl and coat. The genial landlord or landlady
would have been seen directing operations in the hall.   There would
have been a goodly display of cold meats, game pies, cheese and pastries
on view in the glazed cupboard in the hall. The coffee room or the dining
parlour would have revealed a central table of enormous size with viands
on dishes and knives and forks in readiness. The dinner would have been
served with expedition and the head waiter would have made it his
business to see that no delay occurred in satisfying the guests and getting
the reckoning paid. We have a suspicion—it is a just one—that in doubtful
weather every effort was made by the landlord to persuade the passenger
to break the journey and to continue the next day, " When the weather
was sure to improve."   If, as Oliver Goldsmith recounts in " She Stoops
to Conquer," travellers of an earlier day had on some occasions mistaken
old roadside houses for inns (Fig. 182), there was little danger of the
repetition of such mistakes in the year 1800. The romance of road
travelling about which we read so much to-day, a century and a quarter
since was entering upon its final stage. Travellers could count on reaching
their destination with certainty and on time. The inns, which then served
much the same purpose as the main line junctions of to-day, were scenes
of the greatest activity. Moreover, the old class distinctions were
fast disappearing. It is true that the nobility scorned to travel by the
public stage, but professional men, clergy, soldiers and others looked
upon the reputable inn as a home from home. Even Royalty would
stop the night at a good inn and all unknowingly found a local tradition.
We have the authority of Joseph Farington for the accommodation
of the inns of the late eighteenth and early nineteenth centuries.   We

read of George Morland's delight in the high class house as in the tavern and the alehouse (Figs. 228, 256). It was the spirit of adventure that prompted Rowlandson to order the " Chaise " to the door preparatory to starting on one of his larks through the countryside. Coaching then was a sport as well as being a means of speedy communication between towns. This is the period of Cary's and Paterson's road-books, when the middle classes formed the bulk of the stage coach traffic, and the roads teemed with all sorts of wheeled carriages ranging from the Berlin to the lumbering stage waggon which was used to run between Exeter and London or from London to York. The earlier inns of the eighteenth century were now beginning to be regarded by travellers as antiquated and out of date. In response to the development of inter-course between London and the country towns many new inns were built and existing ones remodelled and finished almost regardless of cost, and this while the country was engaged in the Napoleonic Wars. Although at this time the demand was for greater comfort and elegance, the exteriors of the inns became more and more severe, for the builders and designers, anxious to please the proprietors, strove to make the plain fronts imposing in scale if not in the display of ornament.

The old alehouses have the original settles and tables it is true, but the great houses have to be content with a few specimens of the age of mahogany and not a light load of ponderous Victorian sideboards, chairs, tables and mirrors. We have become suspicious of furniture planted in some inns. *The Royal Hotel* at Southend a few years since could show some remarkable specimens of Regency moveables that had been in position since Royalty once lodged in a house almost adjoining. The Chippendale chairs at the Swan in Bedford are the originals. *The Kings Arms* at Christchurch (Figs. 114, 123) has a few good pieces which are original, and the side tables at *The Swan*, Newport Pagnell, are without compeer. *The Lygon Arms* at Broadway (Figs. 85, 95) is a veritable museum, but no doubt some of the pieces have been collected.

No definite system of planning seems to have been adhered to through the centuries for inns other than to provide a yard around which were grouped sets of lodgings and a further yard for stabling and waggons. *The Haycock* at Wansford (Figs. 20-22) is a fine example of late seventeenth century planning on the lines of a mansion. The old inns of London consisted in the main of a block facing the street with an entry to a courtyard within, the front part of the house being reserved for sitting-rooms and eating parlours. The problem of the

Georgian builders was to provide easy ingress through an arched entry
for coaches, which made their way out through a gate in the further
yard.   To right or left of this entry, which varied according to circum-
stance, there was generally a large room where coach passengers could
dine ; to the left was the coach office and a passage connecting with
the bar and the coffee room.   The drawing room was on the first floor.
This arrangement was generally followed in all parts of the country.
The early nineteenth century inn, such as *The Stamford Hotel* (Fig. 116),
which was planned by John Linnell Bond, has all the characteristics
of a mansion.   Here is to be seen a vaulted vestibule at the centre
with a view of a geometrical staircase gracefully ascending two flights,
and lit from the top by a domed light.   To the left and right of the
vestibule are respectively the coffee room and a private sitting room.
On the left of the staircase is the office with its glazed screen.   The
assembly room is on the first floor.   The arched entry for coaches is
on the extreme left of the façade, and this leads to a rectangular courtyard, or rather series of yards, about the greater of which stand the
heavy stone buildings of the early eighteenth century which, heavily
girt with a modillion cornice, have the air of being beetle-browed.
One feels on viewing the scene within the courtyard that one has been
transported from the day when Sir Walter Scott saw the front of the
building completed to that earlier time of York and London travelling
known to Defoe.   From 1800 to 1820 the style of the coaching inn
changed outwardly.   There had been a hint of such development in
the design of *The George* at Grantham (Fig. 31) as early as the year
1789.   There were now to be seen surface departures as well as alterations
in the character of porches and arched entries which give the works
of the early nineteenth century that definite modern stamp that in
turn heralds the coming of the age of steam.   A typical early nineteenth
century inn is *The Grosvenor* at Shaftesbury, which in design combines
a certain classic formality with such picturesque features as diminutive
windows on the ground floor and a Tuscan order of columns which
seem to be able just to sustain the load placed on them.   In Exeter
the London Inn, built in 1810, can be taken as a period type.   This
house is finely proportioned ; the windows to the ground storey are
arched, the portico is frankly Greek, and the interior is distinguished
for the elegance of the joinery and the good quality of the ironmongery.
It was about this time, or a little earlier, that *The Old Courtenay Arms*
at Star Cross received the addition of the segmental bow to the wing
which faces the river Exe.   Many of the larger inns, such as *The Royal*

Fig. 103. The Front.

Fig. 104. The Courtyard.

THE GEORGE, STAMFORD.

FIG. 106. THE TALBOT, TOWCESTER, NORTHANTS.

FIG. 105. GEORGIAN ADDITIONS, ANGEL, GRANTHAM.
(v. also Figs. 13 and 14.)

Fig. 107. A COACHING BREAKFAST, THE BULL, REDBOURN, HERTFORDSHIRE. (J. Pollard.)

FIG. 108. THE BULL, ROYSTON, HERTFORDSHIRE. (Hanslip Fletcher, del.)

FIG. 109. THE RED LION, HATFIELD.

FIG. 110. On a Devon Quay, Topsham, Exe Estuary.

FIG. 111. The Angel, Henley-on-Thames.

WATERSIDE INNS.

FIG. 112. AN INN KITCHEN, LATE XVIIITH CENTURY. (T. Rowlandson.)

FIG. 113. DEPARTURE OF THE FLEET, PORTSMOUTH. (T. Rowlandson.)

FIG. 114. KING'S ARMS, CHRISTCHURCH, HAMPSHIRE.

FIG. 115. THE BULL, ROCHESTER.

FIG. 117. THE SWAN, BEDFORD. (Henry Halland, Architect.)

FIG. 116. THE STAMFORD HOTEL, STAMFORD.

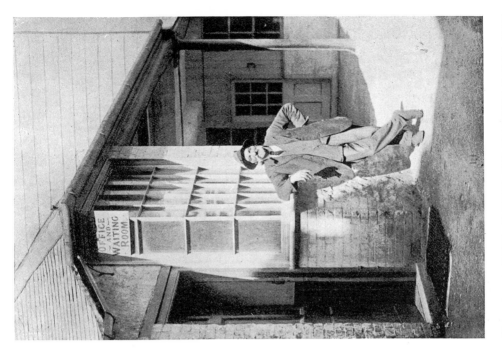

Fig. 119. PARCEL OFFICE AND WAITING ROOM, THE KING'S ARMS, DORCHESTER.

Fig. 118. DOOR IN THE LOUNGE, THE KING'S ARMS, DORCHESTER. (v. also Fig. 266.)

FIG. 120.   THE INN YARD DURING A FIRE.   (Rowlandson and Malton.)

Fig. 121. DAMP SHEETS. (T. Rowlandson.)

FIG. 122. A WELL-FOUND KITCHEN OF A HUNDRED YEARS AGO. (G. Scharf, del.)

FIG. 123. FIREPLACE IN THE LOUNGE, THE KING'S ARMS, CHRISTCHURCH.

Fig. 124. A COFFEE HOUSE IN FITZROY SQUARE, ABOUT 1830. (G. Scharf del.)

Fig. 125. SANDERS' COFFEE AND EATING HOUSE, NEWGATE STREET.
(G. Scharf del.)

FIG. 126. A MEET AT THE PLUME OF FEATHERS, PRINCETOWN, DARTMOOR.

FIG. 127 AT SHILLINGFORD BRIDGE, ON THAMES.

at Plymouth, built by John Foulston, *The Stamford Hotel* by John Linnel Bond (Fig. 116), Webbs at Liskeard, *The White Lion* at Upton-on-Severn, *The Cups* at Lyme Regis, and others, including *The Royal* at Falmouth, became quite frankly semi-official buildings in their brave display of Ionic and Corinthian trimmings, that is to say as far as architectural display is concerned. There are many such inns, which at this time were named hotels, well worthy of study, for they reflect the social customs of the early nineteenth century just as the half-timbered buildings of the Middle Ages serve as an index to the time of the Plantagenets and Tudors.

Few there are who would pass Elliot's *Royal Hotel* at Devonport without a thought of the officers of Nelson's time and the innovations wrought by Seppings to the wooden battleships when he introduced the circular stem in his designs. Of Regency inns much could be written. There is *The Golden Cross* in London, *The Seven Stars* at Totnes, *The Regent* at Leamington Spa and *The Queen's* at Cheltenham. At Honiton in Devonshire is Banfield's *Dolphin*, with the adjoining Assembly Rooms sporting like the dolphin with head somewhat higher and larger than the tail. The period of the Regency was an age of stucco. It was an age of Corinthian splendour, when gold leaf was used profusely to decorate plaster ornament ; an age of smartness and white paint : but builders, despite their predilection for sham surfaces, knew the values of proportion, " and 'fore gad, sirs," that was a point in their favour. One of the best known of Regency hotels is *The Old Ship* at Brighton, the exterior portion, namely the four-storeyed bays and the Doric portico of the original house, affording a faithful account of its lineage. But honest brickwork was by no means neglected, as is seen in *The Antelope* in Dorchester, built as a rival to the bucolic *King's Arms* (Figs. 118, 119, 266). The Antelope as a hostelry goes back to mediæval times. There are panelled rooms of the seventeenth century and one in which tradition asserts Judge Jefferies held his assize of ill fame in 1685, when he condemned 200 of Monmouth's followers to death. Throughout the eighteenth century this house shared with The King's Arms the reputation of being the best posting house in Dorset. Finally, in 1815, it was remodelled to accord with the smart passenger coaches that plied in this particular route between London and Exeter, for the travelling public demanded modern accommodation in sympathy with the new-fangled springing, safety hubs and reading lamps within the coaches. At this time *The Bull* at Rochester (Fig. 115) made its debut as a new hostelry, and the staircase and Assembly Room were established in readiness for the famous meeting of Jingle and Dr. Slammer. As we write so the inns we have enjoyed continue to appear. They are extraordinarily diverse: There is a mental picture of *The Star and Garter* at Andover, the inn at Stockbridge, the stone front of *The Bull* at Cambridge, the façade of *The Great White Horse* at Ipswich and the stuccoed conventions of the private hotels of Clifton. Finally we reach the period when the locomotive came in and the coach went off the roads. Old prints and engravings of the Regency are continually discovered, telling of the interest of journeys prior to the time when the system of travel underwent the change which ruined many honest landlords and coach proprietors. The old *Royal Western Hotel* at Bristol, which was built in the 'forties of the last century, is a case in point. The advertisement of this house has all the flavour of the eighteenth century, with, of course, certain additions which are entitled to be thought modern :—

HAM'S ROYAL WESTERN HOTEL,

NEW COLLEGE GREEN, BRISTOL,

Offers superior accommodation in Suites of Apartments handsomely fitted up and combining every comfort for Families, with Coffee and Commercial Rooms not surpassed by any Houses in the Kingdom, to which the Travelling Community are respectfully solicited.

BATHS, WARM, COLD, VAPOUR AND SHOWER, IN THE HOUSE.

Omnibuses to and from every Train.

R. P. HAM, *Proprietor,*
Turtle and Wine Merchant.

THE WHITE HORSE, HOCKLIFFE, BEDFORDSHIRE.
Hugh Mottram, A.R.I.B.A., del.

CHAPTER IV

OLD LONDON INNS

A HUNDRED years in the life of the metropolis has wrought many changes, but none so sweeping as the passing of her ancient inns. There are, it is true, a few survivals, so precious as to have acquired a new importance. Old names and signs have lingered on, and by some strange trick topographical distinctions of plan have become bonded with the fabric of the city. In the provinces can be seen the hostelries of the past. They are among the familiar sights, and to many are evidence that at one time London could show inns of equal, if not of greater, interest ; for time was when the whole range of county towns had special inns of call in the metropolis which, to travellers to and from the shires, were more than friendly. It is to London, then, that we must devote attention to complete the survey of social life and inter-course that flourished in other days.

To Londoners the scenery is so familiar that few trouble to acquire a taste for historical facts. Steam has provided means of escape from closely-packed streets, the revival of the road has placed obscure country towns within a few hours journey. The London inn, therefore, has lost its meaning, and in this essential the city is not the place it was even half a century since. In spite of the changes, the number of old inns and taverns is not inconsiderable. The antiquary well versed in historical records finds not a little difficulty in attempting a recon-struction of the past, but he can do little more than generalise on the secret of the life that has gone. Every day fresh surprises are encountered. Each excavation made with pick and shovel for the foundations of a new building in the city turns up relics in the form of drinking vessels, broken tobacco pipes, and tokens proving that at one time a tavern stood on the site. By some strange chance it has happened that inns renowned before the coming of steam have been acquired by the railway companies that usurped their right to be ; in others that the business of a once famous carrier has been merged into that of a modern transport company.

In outward appearance the city has changed, but if its streets are studied it will be found that the linear dimensions of the inn, and court-yard, with the entries and blind alley-ways, have a curious habit of asserting themselves when all else has gone. Apart from the inns still existing, which to the majority may or may not be familiar, there are many ancient structures which have been adapted to a different purpose. The City itself, as already pointed out, while rich in signs and nomenclature, with a fair sprinkling of coffee houses, has little to show of inns of the old type. Outside the ancient boundaries there are, happily, more relics. In Whitechapel stand in close order, as if for mutual protection, the gabled fronts, some of which were taverns that greeted the waggoner from Harwich or Ely (Fig. 40). There are the courts of Aldersgate and John Street, Clerkenwell (Fig. 128), that once echoed to the broad-wheeled stage-waggons from the Midland shires. Holborn can show offsets from its breadth that at one time helped its reputation as an inn centre. And the same can be said of Newgate Street. It is Southwark that expresses more directly former custom in the matter of relics and the shape of inn yards. London, then, has changed outwardly. It is a mood responding to her life-blood, but she conceals nothing from her disciples. To the casual her past is a secret ; to the enquirer it is a mirage. The fascination to all is the sphinx-like attitude of the ancient city, her merciless non-chalance, the changes wrought by time, and the ant-like activities of her people.

It would be a difficult task to undertake a perambulation of the streets without some knowledge of the records of the venerable Stow, or of his successors, Strype, Maitland or Lambert. It is essential to carry in the mind memories of seventeenth century woodcuts, of the etchings made by Wenceslaus Hollar (Fig. 136), of Hogarth engravings (Figs. 165, 199), of the prints published by Sayer and Bowles (Fig. 30), as well as those later pictures by Shotter Boys. We should be doubly equipped for our quest if we could carry in our minds the varying aspects of London during the last three centuries ; in other words, to see the buildings and the streets, first in wood engravings, later in the tones of aquatint and friendly lithograph, then as steel engravings. It will be necessary to know the old maps of London and Westminster, made before and after the Fire, to be familiar with the written word of those famous Londoners to whom London was so vivid, so kind and so mysterious. The architect is able to scent old buildings without reference to parchment or print. It is part of his training, but he is apt to ignore the poetry of the past and to be carried away with enthusiasm for detail. The amateur, on the other hand, has the power, if he will only employ it, of seeing things in a dispassionate way.

Whatever the future may hold, it is the past that enchains us. It needs much unravelling, and when everything seems to conspire to destroy its concrete symbols, it appears more valuable. The inns are, for the most part, buried in the dust of old London. To include even a partial account of their story is akin to having at one's disposal an authentic history with the opening chapter missing.

It is to the country inns we must turn for a general idea of the aspect of the vanished inns of London Town. It is fitting, in any description of the old inns of London, that those of Southwark should provide material for its start. At a mile south of London Bridge stood the old *Elephant and Castle*, which every traveller in the coaching days knew as a prominent landmark. The building drawn by Rowlandson (Fig. 38) came into existence probably about the year 1674. It was rebuilt in 1824, and forms the subject of one of a fine series of coaching prints (Fig. 131). The sign may have been taken from the Cutlers' Company. The present tavern is an entirely new structure.

Southwark has always been noted for its inns, which for centuries outnumbered the houses, shops and tenements. Being on the high road to Canterbury and Dover, it was the rendezvous for the stage waggons to and from the southern counties and gave facilities for goods to be unloaded near the City without the trouble of crossing London Bridge. A State Paper of 1619 gives the information that the borough " consists chiefly of inn-keepers." Stow in his Survey of 1598 says : " From thence (the Marshalsea) toward London Bridge on the same side be many fair inns for the receipt of travellers ; by these signs : *The Spurre, Christopher, Bull, Queen's Head, Tabard, George, White Hart, King's Head.*" In the Record Office is a map showing most of the Southwark inns. They were grouped together on the east side of what is now the Borough High Street. These inns usually had a gateway shutting off the courtyard from the street, which was closed at night. After passing through the gateway a full perspective of the yard was seen, with the galleries and the doors of the rooms where the guests were housed (Figs. 134, 141 and 148). At the back of the first courtyard was a larger yard with the stabling and other tenements. In most cases there was an outlet to a street at the back to enable waggons to pass through.

One of the largest of the Southwark inns was *The White Hart* which may have been built in the fourteenth century, the sign being derived from the badge of Richard II. Jack Cade made it his headquarters in the summer of 1450. In 1529 the inn is heard of again through a message sent to Thomas Cromwell, asking for an interview at the White Hart. In 1669 the back part of the inn was destroyed by fire, and in 1676, during the fire which raged in Southwark, when five hundred houses were destroyed, the White Hart shared the general fate. It was one of the first to be rebuilt. Strype, writing in 1720, describes it " as very large and of a considerable trade "—and from that time until the opening years of the last century it continued to be patronised by Kentish travellers. It was then, as described by Charles Dickens in " Pickwick," " a double tier of bedroom galleries, with old clumsy balustrades run round two sides of the straggling area, and a double row of bells to correspond, sheltered from the weather by a little sloping roof, hung over the door leading to the bar and coffee room. Two or three gigs and chaise carts were wheeled up under different little sheds and penthouses ; and the occasional heavy tread of a carthorse or rattling of a chain at the farther end of the yard announced to anybody who cared about the matter that the stable lay in that direction. When we add that a few boys in smock frocks were lying asleep on heavy packages, woolpacks and other articles that were scattered about on heaps of straw, we have described as fully as need be the general appearance of the yard of the White Hart Inn, High Street, Borough, on the particular morning in question." After 1865 the south side of the building was rebuilt and the old galleries were let out as tenements, and in 1889 the old remains finally disappeared.

The Tabard (Fig. 140), selected by Chaucer as the starting place for his Canterbury Pilgrims, is the most famous of the Southwark inns.

> " Byfel that in that sesoun on a day
>   In Southwark at the Tabard as I lay."

Chaucer gives the name of the landlord, Henry Bailly, who represented Southwark at the Parliament held at Westminster in 1376. The antiquity of the house is beyond doubt. In 1304 the Abbot and Convent of Hythe purchased here from William de Lategareshall two houses, held of the Archbishop of Canterbury. On this site the Abbot built himself a town dwelling and at the same time probably an hostelry for travellers. Stow mentions these facts. A celebrated London antiquary, the late Mr. G. Rutter Fletcher, discovered a lease of the Tabard dated 1st of April, 31 Henry VIII. Its chief interest is in the enumeration of the rooms and their fixtures. The sign of the Tabard, taken, as some think, from the sleeveless coat worn by the heralds, was continued to the end of the sixteenth century, when it was changed to *The Talbot*. Additions were made to the building at the close of the sixteenth century ; at the time of the 1676 fire The Talbot and its outbuildings were destroyed. It was shortly afterward rebuilt in Carolean taste (Fig. 140), following the old plan, and so it continued till 1876.

What is left of *The George Inn* (Figs. 133 and 134)* stands between the sites of *The Tabard* and *The White Hart*. Old records show that the building came into being in the early part of the sixteenth century. In 1558 it was owned by Humfrey. Collet, who had been member of Parliament for Southwark. It also appears that the inn was rebuilt of brick and timber during the first quarter of the seventeenth century. Fire seems to have been the chief enemy of the Southwark inns. In 1670 the George was partly burnt and suffered the fate of the Talbot in the fire of 1676. The fragment now remaining dates from this time. The George was famous throughout Kent and Sussex as a coaching and carriers' inn, and one may even now chance upon a stray advertisement in Canterbury and Tunbridge Wells giving notice of the departure of stage waggons to the George at Southwark. After 1889 the yard was leased to the Great Northern Railway Company, and thus comparatively late in its career the inn has been associated with modern methods of travel. One enters the inn yard with pleasurable anticipation ; there is fortunately sufficient of the old building remaining to carry the mind back to the days of its former prosperity. There are the sagging galleries, the heavily-sashed windows and the old glass in the squares. The rooms are panelled. In the dining-room are the pews, and the bar is typical. It is also significant that the house is still patronised by men of Kent who frequent the hop and vegetable market. Here we can obtain old English fare, and, heedless of the beat of London, commune with the ghostly frequenters to whom the place was at one time a reality. Fortunate is Southwark in her possessions, for she holds in this fragment a key to the aspect of her many vanished inns, as well as to the character of the inns across London Bridge that served to receive travellers from the North. *The Nag's Head* inn is shown on a map of Southwark, dated 1542, as *The Horse Hed*. Strype refers to the building in 1720 as " old and sorry with inhabitants answerable." Andrew Ducrow, the equestrian performer, is said to have been born here in 1796. George Coleman the younger, in his *Poor Gentleman*, a comedy produced at Covent Garden in 1801, makes a farmer say : " I be come from Lunnon,

---

* Fully illustrated in the plates of the Society for Photographing Relics of Old London, a very valuable record of old London inns generally.

you see.   I warrant I smell of smoke, like the Nag's Head chimney in
the Borough."   During the first half of the nineteenth century the
business lingered on, some assemblies were held in the large room, and
the reputation of the house was fair.   Eventually its career as an inn
closed and the yard came into the possession of the Great Western Railway.

Another inn of repute amongst carriers was the old *King's Head*
(Fig. 135), originally called *The Pope's Head*, a name changed after the
Reformation.   In 1588 the house came into the possession of the Humble
family.   It was burned in the fire of 1676, rebuilt soon after, and lasted
until 1885.   It is recorded that the sign was a well-painted half-length
of Henry VIII, as seen in the illustration.

The Queen's Head (Fig. 143) stood on the site of a house called
The Crowned or Cross Keys, a place belonging to the Poynings family.
At one time a store place for the King's harness, it passed into the hands
of Richard Westray, who bequeathed the property to his wife Joan.
In 1634 we find the house called the Queen's Head, the owner being
the celebrated John Harvard, of Emmanuel College, Cambridge, who
eventually journeyed to America and gave his name to the Massachusetts
University.   Taylor, the water-poet, tells us that the house was much
frequented by carriers.   By good fortune the house escaped the fire
of 1676.   In 1856 the main building was pulled down and was then
found to be of timber construction of Tudor date.   The galleried portion
of the inn survived until twenty years ago.   There is another inn on
the south side of the Thames which can claim to be of remote origin,
and that is *The Bricklayers' Arms*, which an old writer states to have
been " a vast hostel on the old road from Kent into Southwark, about
two-thirds of a league from the Bridge across the Thames."   When
the inn received its name is not to be ascertained ; it was prior to its
rebuilding in 1881 a timber frame building, so it is more than probable
that its name was given to it after the Fire of London, when brick building
became general.

In the City the sites of the famous inns can be distinguished in one
of two ways, namely, by the retention of a courtyard with an arched
entry from the street, or by a legend cut in stone or some other record
such as nomenclature.   The yard of *The Swan with Two Necks*, in Lad
Lane, is a well-known example ; it was owned by the famed William
Chaplin, at one time the foremost coach proprietor in London ; his trade
card is seen in Fig 221.   He it was who joined with Horne after the coming
of the railroad to develop the carrying business on the old ground.   Lad
Lane is now part of Gresham Street.

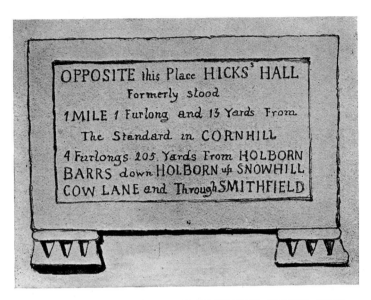

FIG. 128. TABLET TO COMMEMORATE HICK'S HALL, CLERKENWELL (the early Sessions House), THE STARTING POINT OF MILESTONES.

FIG. 129. PALACE YARD, WESTMINSTER, WITH COACHES, MID. XVIIth CENT.
(Wencelaus Hollar, sc.)

FIG. 130. THE BELL, KILBURN, 1789. (Rathbone del.)

FIG. 131. THE ELEPHANT AND CASTLE, S.E., ABOUT 1820. (— Jones, ag.)
(v. also Fig. 38.)

FIG. 132. XVIITH CENTURY CHIMNEYPIECE IN THE BAPTIST'S HEAD, CLERKENWELL. (Now destroyed.) (J. Wykeham Archer, del.)

FIG. 133. A CORNER IN THE GEORGE, SOUTHWARK.

142

FIG. 135. THE KING'S HEAD, SOUTHWARK. (T. H. Shepherd, del.)

FIG. 134. THE GEORGE, SOUTHWARK. (T. H. Shepherd, del.)
(v. also Fig. 133.)

Fifty years ago there was standing in Warwick Lane one of the most interesting inns of central London, *The Oxford Arms*, shown in Figs. 42, 144. It was approached by a passage from Warwick Lane. Bounded on the West by the site of the old London Wall, on the South it reached to Amen Corner. From its picturesque galleries could be seen the towering mass of St. Paul's, as shown in the series of the Society for Photographing Relics of Old London. Here could be conjured up the spirit of London as Wren knew it. The house was rebuilt after the Fire, and conformed to the species of galleried courtyard made familiar by the fragment by the George in Southwark. But this house was of greater pretentions. An advertisement in the " London Gazette " for March, 1672-73, reads : " These are to give notice that Edward Bartlett, Oxford carrier, hath removed his inn in London from *The Swan* at Holborn Bridge, to *The Oxford Arms*, in Warwick Lane, where he did inn before the Fire, his coaches and waggons going forth on their usual days, Mondays, Wednesdays and Fridays. He hath also a hearse and all things convenient to carry a Corps to any part of England." At the time of Waterloo the Oxford Arms was owned by Edward Sherman, whose chief centre for coaching traffic was the Bull and Mouth, St. Martin's-le-Grand (Fig. 141). It was Sherman who ran certain of the coaches on the Chester Road. In 1868 some of the rooms were let as tenements, but the carriers' business survived, long distance waggons and carts still making the journey to Oxford and places on the Western roads. In 1875, the old buildings were demolished.

There was another galleried inn, *The Bell*, on the east side of Warwick Lane, where Archbishop Leighton died in 1684, as Burnet states ; he had often said that " if he were to choose a place to die in it should be an Inn ; it looked like a pilgrim's going home, to whom this world was all as an Inn, and who was weary of the noise and confusion in it."

Few old prints remain to show the aspect of the Belle Sauvage, on Ludgate Hill. Even the engravings of London, published by Boydell, do not record this interesting hostelry. We have, therefore, to rely on the accurate draughtsmanship of Shepherd for our ideas of the inn courtyard. The entry from Ludgate Hill still remains and so does some portion of the courtyard. It was one of the most important of London inns ; in its palmy days travellers could lodge almost beneath the west front of St. Paul's, and it was on this account more popular than the inns in Warwick Lane. It is on record that one William Lawton was sentenced in the reign of Richard II to stand for an hour in the pillory for trying to obtain by means of a forged letter twenty shillings from William Savage, of Fleet Street, in the parish of St. Bridget.   Whether this William Savage had anything to do with the inn remains in doubt.   In 1453, during the reign of Henry VI, a church roll notices the bequest of John French to his mother, Joan French, widow, of " *Savage's Inn*," otherwise called the " *Bell in the Hoop*," in the parish of St. Bride's.   Stow mentions a Mrs. Savage as having given the inn to the Cutlers' Company, but this is uncertain.   In 1568 one John Craythorne gave the reversion of the Belle Sauvage to the Cutlers' Company, with certain conditions to be observed.   In 1584 (9) the inn was described as "*Ye Belle Savage*."   Landlord's tokens of 1648 and 1672 show an Indian woman holding a bow and arrow.   The sign in the reign of Queen Anne was a savage man standing by a bell.   The question to be decided is whether the name was derived from the original landlady, Isabel (Bel) Savage, or the sign of the Bell and Savage, or as the " Spectator " alleges, from La Belle Sauvage.   In Elizabeth's time the strolling actors and mummers, as was the custom, performed in inn yards, and it is on record that the inn on Ludgate Hill was a favourite place for such performances.   Here Banks exhibited his horse, Marocco, which suffered with his master the fate of burning for witchcraft at Rome.   It is said, too, that Grinling Gibbons lived in one of the houses in front of the inn and exhibited, as a kind of advertisement, a pot of flowers carved in wood, which stood outside his window and shook surprisingly with the motion of the coaches that passed beneath.   If either of the Wellers could return to Ludgate Hill, they would be shocked to find their familiar haunt swept away.   Originally the inn consisted of two courts.   Into the outer one of these the archway from Ludgate Hill led.   At one time the first court contained private houses.   The inn stood round an inner court entered by a second archway.   Over the brick archway to the street was placed the sign of the Bell, which faced the traveller as he was warned to mind his head on departure. From Shepherd's drawing in the Crace collection can be gleaned the architectural treatment of the galleried courtyard whence guests and chambermaids viewed the passengers arriving and departing.   There is a lithograph by Pollard, published in 1828, showing the crack Cambridge coach, the Star, making its way from the entry up Ludgate Hill.   The leaders and wheelers are stepping forth to their task, there is a full complement of passengers inside and outside, and the turnout is as spick and span as lithography can make it.   From Pollard's drawing can be seen the names of the towns served by the coaches in the Western counties, westerly to Bath, Exeter and Plymouth, and northerly to

Coventry, Carlisle and Manchester. The sign of the famous *Bull and Mouth* at St. Martin's-le-Grand is now preserved in the Guildhall Museum (Fig. 195). It is supposed to represent Milo, the Cretonian, who slew an ox with his fist and ate it up at one meal.

> " Milo the Cretonian
> An ox slew with his fist
> And ate it up at one meal,
> Ye Gods ! What a glorious twist ! "

The capacity of the legendary Milo to make a mouthful bears no comparison to the capacity of the inn yard of this famous hostelry, for it ranked as the largest in London and could hold thirty coaches. The original name, as mentioned in a preceding chapter, was Boulogne Mouth, which became corrupted to Bull and Mouth. The drawings of the hostelry made when it was a going concern (Fig. 141) show it as a late seventeenth century building standing foursquare about the courtyard. It had three tiers of galleries finished with a number of blind gables of steep pitch, which gave the place a conventual air. To the left of the arched entry were the coffee room and an enclosed staircase leading, under cover, to the open galleries. Every Monday twenty-one coaches left the yard and made room for a similar number arriving. The coaches from the Bull and Mouth served the towns on the north-western roads as far as Carlisle and Glasgow, as well as to Liverpool, Manchester, Holyhead and other places in North Wales. It was the Euston of the era of road travel. The influence of association is partly explained by the fact that when the Post Office authorities decided to move from Lombard Street they selected a site at St. Martin's-le-Grand as near the private coach yard as possible. It is also significant that Manchester men made the Bull and Mouth their stopping place in London, and when the Queen's Hotel was built on the old site in 1830 the customers transferred their affections to the new house.

The Bull Inn, Bishopsgate Street, has an interest which is associated with the eastern roads, and, strange to say, it is still advertised at Ely as a place of call for stage-waggons (Fig. 146). It was here that Burbage and his group of players obtained a patent from Queen Elizabeth for erecting a theatre. It is also recorded that Anthony Bacon, the brother of Francis, lived in his youth under the watchful eye of his mother in a house not far from the Bull Inn, and that this lady dreaded the baneful effect of the plays and interludes. Another famous character well known at the Bull, as he was on the road between **London** and **Cambridge**, and in the University City, was Thomas Hobson, the carrier, whose memory has been kept green by Milton.

> " ON THE UNIVERSITY CARRIER, WHO SICKENED IN THE TIME OF THE VACANCY, BEING FORBID TO GO TO LONDON, BY REASON OF THE PLAGUE.
>
> " *Here lies old Hobson ; Death hath broke his girt,*
> *And here, alas ! hath laid him in the dirt ;*
> *Or else, the ways being foul, twenty to one,*
> *He's here stuck in a slough, and overthrown.*
> *'Twas such a shifter, that if truth were known,*
> *Death was half glad, when he got him down;*
> *For he had, any time these ten years full,*
> *Dodg'd with him, betwixt Cambridge and the Bull ;*
> *And surely Death could never have prevailed,*
> *Had not his weekly course of carriage fail'd ;*
> *But lately finding him so long at home,*
> *And thinking now his journey's end was come,*
> *And that he had ta'en up his latest inn,*
> *In the kind office of a chamberlain*
> *Shew'd him his room, where he must lodge that night,*
> *Pull'd off his boots, and took away the light ;*
> *If any ask for him, it shall be said,*
> *' Hobson has supt, and's newly gone to bed.' "*

It is recorded that there was a painted figure of Hobson on one of the prominent walls of the inn showing the old carrier with a hundred-pound bag under his arm and on the bag was inscribed, " The fruitful mother of a hundred more." It was within the Bull that Van Horn, a celebrated guest, is said to have drunk 35,680 bottles of wine. It would be interesting to locate this gentleman's portrait and the parchment certificate of his prowess as a toper.

Another fine inn was *The Four Swans* (Fig. 139). This was in part a three-galleried house which had been rebuilt after the Fire. Another Bishopsgate inn, the Green Dragon, from the time of Charles II. onwards was also a rendezvous for carriers. The changes made in the City in the 'seventies swept away many of the associations made famous by the writings of Charles Dickens, but none was more drastic than that by which the building of Holborn Viaduct changed the topography of Holborn Hill. In vain does the student of old London look for that erstwhile renowned hostelry, *The Saracen's Head*, one of the oldest in London to bear the sign. It was mentioned by Stow as " a fair large inn for receipt of travellers," that " hath to sign the ' Saracen's

Head.'" From old drawings we know it to have been built of brick, the original work long obscured by a dressing of Stuart detail and galleries of the late seventeenth century. This inn had an especial

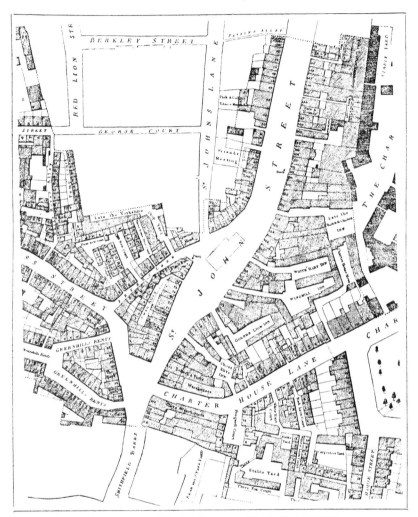

FIG. 136.—PART PLAN OF CLERKENWELL,
LATE EIGHTEENTH CENTURY   *Samuel Angell, Sc.*

affinity with coach traffic that made its way northwards through Islington, Highgate and Barnet, to Stamford and York. Not the smart mail coaches, but heavy stage carriages that made the journey with a surprising regularity. All are familiar with the journey made by

Nicholas Nickleby as assistant to Squeers. Dickens describes the coach
yard of *The Saracen's Head Inn,* " with its portals guarded by two
Saracens' heads and shoulders which it was once the pride and glory
of the choice spirits of this Metropolis to pull down at night."   " There
they are, frowning upon you from each side of the gateway, and the inn
itself, garnished with another Saracen's head, frowns upon you from the
top of the yard ; while from the door of the hind boot of all the red
coaches that are standing therein, there glares a small Saracen's head
with a twin expression to the large Saracen's head below, so that the
general appearance of the pile is of the Saracenic order."

There do not appear to have been many " Saracen's Heads " on the
road to York.   There is the famous *Saracen's Head,* now the Pomfret
Arms, at Towcester, on the Holyhead Road (Fig. 86), and the wayside
tavern, *The Swan with Two Necks* at Whetstone, may perhaps record
the fact that certain coaches from William Chaplin's establishment
in Lad Lane changed horses there.

Mention must here be made of two minor inns.   The first is *The
White Hart,* Bishopsgate (Fig. 152), which was in existence as early as
1426.   It is conjectured that at one time this inn formed part of the
Bethlehem Priory, and was the hostel for the reception of pilgrims
and other guests ; eventually it became recognised as " a fair inn for the
receipt of travellers."   The other is an hostelry which was standing
up to a few years back, the White Horse, in Fetter Lane (Fig. 167),
a house with three gables of seventeenth century character.   The coach
yard extended as far back as Barnard's Inn.   There is an etching by
Mr. Hanslip Fletcher, made before this house was demolished, which
shows the lower part converted to shops.   It is on record that Titus
Oates had five Catholic lords committed to the Tower for an alleged
traitorous consultation within this inn.

The Bell, in Holborn, which was demolished in 1897 (Fig. 137),
was at one time frequented by carriers from Buckinghamshire.   It
eventually became a coaching house of importance, and in 1836 was
owned by the Hornes, who at that time, as coach proprietors, were rivalled
only by Chaplin.   This inn differed but little from the galleried houses
already described.   Until late in the 'sixties there was a road carrier from
the Bell to Uxbridge, the Chalfonts, Amersham and Wendover.   *The
Black Bull* adjoined *The Bell* ; it was here that Dickens pictured Sairey
Gamp and Betsy Prig ministering to Mr. Lewsome.   Almost opposite
to these inns was the Black Swan, which had the distinction as early
as 1706 of advertising a coach that conveyed passengers from there

at five o'clock in the morning, thrice weekly, to the Black Swan at York in four days, "if God permits." The inns of Holborn, taken as a whole, were very minor concerns, and will not bear comparison with the more central coaching houses of the eighteenth and early nineteenth centuries.

Gradually, as the subject is investigated, the different centres from which coach traffic started out from London to join the highways are brought into prominence. We have referred to *La Belle Sauvage* as being the starting point for some of the west-bound coaches. Another old inn which has recently been cleared away, at least all that remained of its early Victorian splendour, is *The Bolt in Tun*, Fleet Street. It is said that this inn formed part of, or belonged to, the Carmelite Priory. Carey's "Travelling Companion" shows that in the days of the Regency the number of coaches

FIG. 137.—THE BELL, HOLBORN, 1894.

Roland W. Paul, del.

starting from here to the West Country, as well as the towns of north-eastern England, was twenty-six. It had a "booking-office" for passengers which, in course of time, became a railway booking-office for parcels, and the proprietors at one time were

" Robert Gray and Moses Pickwick & Co."   It is more than likely
that Dickens took the name of Pickwick from the notice displayed
in the booking-office.   He may have had knowledge of the village of
Pickwick, near Bath, and have taken his idea from the association of
the names, as well as from the fact that the firm's name was painted
on certain Bath coaches.   Be this as it may, the chain of inns serving
the West Country indubitably began at the foot of Ludgate Hill and
continued to Charing Cross and *The White Horse Cellar* in Piccadilly.

Charing Cross had its coaching terminus in days long anterior to
the age of steam.   This was the famous Georgian inn known as *The
Golden Cross* (Fig. 153), a five-storeyed house of brick with sashed shop-
fronts on either side of the coach entry.   In the hey-day of its prosperity,
long before Smirke rebuilt the house as a hotel, it was known affectionately
among travellers as The Bull and Mouth of the west.   Until late in
the eighteenth century it had an exterior sign-post and a long water-
trough, evidence of the rurality of the district, so near and yet so far
from the City.   The most superior inn of the early nineteenth century
was *The White Horse Cellar*, in Piccadilly.   This stood close by Arlington
Street.   It was a favourite rendezvous for all good Londoners.   Its
praises have been sung in song and verse, its frequenters have been
described, together with the itinerant merchants who badgered passengers
to buy oranges, penknives and pocket diaries.   On summer evenings,
crowds gathered here to watch the West Country mail coaches depart.
Hazlitt had a warm affection for this sight ; he writes : " The finest
sight in the metropolis is the setting-off of the mail coaches from
Piccadilly.   The horses paw the ground and are impatient to be gone,
as if conscious of the precious burden they convey.   The mail carts
drive up and the transfer of packages is made, and at a given signal
off they start."   He continues : " How we hate the Putney and
Brentford stages that draw up when they are gone !   Some persons think
that the noblest object in Nature is the ship launched on the bosom of
the ocean ; but give me, for my private satisfaction, the mail coaches
that pour down Piccadilly of an evening, tear up the pavement, and
devour the way before them to *The Land's End*."   And so the inns of
old London go out of town with the westerly coaches.   Set back from
the highway are small taverns at Chiswick and Brentford, by Sion House
and Hounslow, marking the preliminary stages of the journey so familiar
to our forbears.   Many of these curious survivals are still serving as
inns, but they have fallen on evil days since all London has gone to
the country.

FIG. 139.

THE FOUR SWANS, BISHOPSGATE. (T. H. Shepherd, del.)

FIG. 138.

THE GRAPES, LIMEHOUSE, FROM THE FORESHORE.

Fig. 140. THE TALBOT, BOROUGH. (T. H. Shepherd, del.)

Fig. 141. THE BULL & MOUTH, ST. MARTIN'S-LE-GRAND. (T. H. Shepherd, del.)

Among the scores of gazetteers and travellers' guides, as well as the few itineraries of travel—the Bradshaws of the past—much information can be gleaned of the inns. As the subject is investigated they start up in a never-ending series, like mendicants claiming recognition. We read of this or that inn in long-forgotten correspondence, such as the private letters of Sir William Chambers, who used to journey at least once a week from Berners Street to his country house at Whitton, or from old diaries we note indignant records regarding the charges and the faulty accommodation. We become aware of that nest of inns in St. John's Street, Clerkenwell (Fig. 136), which were the bournes of stage-waggons from Hertfordshire and Bedfordshire. We linger with curiosity in modern Islington to speculate on the former aspect of this merry village which has never quite lost the reputation for jollity it gained in the days of Queen Elizabeth. Such inns as *The Angel, The Peacock* and *The Queen's Head* (Fig. 74) were recognised stopping places for the northbound coaches. If this part of London is haunted, perhaps in the dead of night, when few people are abroad, the shades of the old hostlers can still be seen standing ready to announce the departure of the York Highflyer, the Stamford Regent, and a score of other crack coaches, once equally renowned. Although the inns have gone, Islington still shows its Georgian brickwork to advantage, and within *The Queen's Head* is still preserved the chimney-piece and panelling which tradition asserts was known to Lord Treasurer Burghley. So much for the main road houses. There remain the interesting taverns of old London for our delectation.

Some survive intact to the smallest detail, others in part, and yet others in name only. It is a curious *melange* of what has been and what has survived. We begin to understand the social life that has gone, to appreciate the village character of the London streets, especially at night when the city holds a different population. There is *The Cheshire Cheese* in Wine Office Court, surely the first of London taverns, if not in antiquity, at least in the wisdom of its settlement. True Londoners gravitate to the Cheese as if by instinct. They are lured there by the very oddities of the place. It is an education in the meaning of London, for there is to be learnt the lesson of dining in the least possible space according to the rites and customs of the past. In no other tavern is tradition so vehemently upheld. There has always been a cat associated with the Cheese. The parrot, too, is a living symbol of the district. The waiters have a proprietary manner that takes the fancy back through the years and gives reality to the portrait

studies of their predecessors on the walls.   The smell of cooking here
is not repellent as in other cases.   The fragrant odours of hot dishes,
of tobacco smoke and sawdust, penetrate every nook, cranny and
corner of this dropsical, lop-sided, corpulent eating-house from the
vaulted cellars to the attic.   Since the rebuilding, after the Fire, to the
present day, the house has been noted for its bill of fare, for its customers
and its seclusion.   The parrot perched on the top of the glazed door
dominates the situation, and when the babel reaches its height cries
shrilly to the cook on the first floor to "put on a chop." When
encouraged to whisper, he breathes impious thoughts against Mr.
Pussyfoot.   It is a study to see the famous pudding served by con-
noisseurs and to watch the frequenters in the bar.   No one dares to
use the word "quaint" within the precincts of the Cheese.   There
is no need for artificial methods to fan enthusiasm for the mellowed
walls, the fitments and the associations.   Doctor Johnson could return
to his accustomed seat without being offended ; Smollett would recognise
the usual attributes of the tavern in the Windsor chairs and the sawdust.
Is it not likely that those who call for tankards secretly desire to be
of the company of Cockney immortals ?   But for all its seclusion there
is a precipitancy in the atmosphere, a call to be up and doing, which
upsets our preconceived notions of eighteenth century ease.   London
awaits without.   There is scarcely time to eat, drink and pay the score,
and as fast as one set of people depart another set is ready for their
places.   If wigs were clapped on to the heads of the people the illusion
would be complete, for here, framed by the heavy sashed windows
of the type familiar to Doctor Johnson at Lichfield, and shown so
accurately by Hogarth in any of his prints of London, is a scene that
might have been witnessed at any London coaching inn in the late
eighteenth century, and at almost any stopping place of importance
on the mail-coach routes.

Fleet Street has its village church and its local shops.   The Cheshire
Cheese is the village tavern, complete to the churchwarden pipes, the
blue crockery and the welcome stiffness of its pew-like seats.

London is a city of surprises, the old is continually being replaced
by the new, yet at times the antique bones of a former age appear with
startling suddenness in the midst of modernity.   There was a vacant
site in Fleet Street in 1925, with the most crazy of hoardings shutting
off the area of desolation within. Above the temporary hoarding,
flying across the frontage, is an oak beam, carved on its surface into
bunches of grapes, which in the days of the Tudors was one of this inn's

minor signs (Fig. 158). This is an interesting survival of the old taverns of London. While on the subject of London taverns, we must speak of *The Cock*, near Temple Bar, in which the old appointments and the fireplace have been assembled ; of *The Mitre* in Mitre Court, of the vanished *Boar's Head* in Cheapside, and of the Castle, extolled by Tarleton. Then there was *Dolly's Tavern*, which stood near *The Castle*, and took its name from Dolly, an old cook of the place, whose portrait was painted by Gainsborough. It seems to have been part of the scheme for old coffee houses and taverns to play hide and seek within courtyards and alleys as far removed from the busyness of the street as was possible. Another famous tavern was *The Three Cranes* in Thames Street, renowned in the reign of James I. Here foregathered the wits contemporary with Ben Jonson, who records his contempt for these usurpers in " Bartholomew Fair," " A pox o' these pretenders to wit, your Three Cranes, Mitre and Mermaid men, not a corn of true thought, not a grain of right mustard amongst them all." Pepys once dined at this tavern with some poor relations, and he records : " We all went over to the Three Cranes Taverne and (though the best room in the house) in such a narrow dogg-hole we were crammed (and I believe we were near forty) and it made me loathe my company and victuals, and a sorry poor dinner it was, too." *The Sir Paul Pindar*, the front of which is now preserved at South Kensington, was originally the town house of a city merchant of that name who had extensive trading connections with Turkey. After 1811 it became a public-house. The coffee houses and taverns of the seventeenth and eighteenth centuries in turn gave place to the clubs of St. James's and Pall Mall, just as a parallel case is afforded by the rise of the family hotels in the West End during the Regency period, when Long's and Thomas's hotels in Berkeley Square had their origin. We have now to summarise the inns and taverns of the villages of outer London of the past, which are now well within the metropolitan area (see, *e.g.*, Fig. 130). *The Monster* tea garden was a popular resort ; it stood on the corner of St. George's Row and Buckingham Palace Road, and probably derived its name from the fact that the land belonged to the Abbot and Monastery, or Convent, of Westminster. It is the only tavern in the country with this sign. *The Sun* Tavern and gardens stood near Buckingham Gate. Other taverns in this district included *Jenny's Whim*, *The Star and Garter*, and *The Orange*. Chelsea had two important taverns in the White Horse, dating from Tudor times, and the Black Lion, which was built in the reign of Charles II. The taverns of Kensington have all been recorded in contemporary drawings.

And so in imagination we can cross the fields to *The Plough* at Kensal Green, which George Morland knew, or revisit the site of *The Bell* at Kilburn (Fig. 130), which, in the days of its prosperity, had two signs, one showing the Bell, and the other, an independent one, with the sign of a bunch of grapes. Another resort of Londoners in the early part of the last century was *The Eyre Arms* in St. John's Wood, in the grounds of which many balloon ascents were made. North Marylebone was long renowned for its tea gardens and alehouses. There were *The Queen's Head and Artichoke, The Jew's Harp, The Farthing Pie House* and *The Yorkshire Stingo*, from whence, in 1829, the first pair of London omnibuses were started by Mr. Shillibeer. There were a host of smaller places of resort on the borders of Marylebone Fields. Camden and Kentish Towns, at one time both hamlets, were a century since considered to be in the country. Many of the old inn names survive in both places. These include *The Mother Red Cap, The Mother Black Cap, The Britannia, The Bedford Arms* and *The Wheatsheaf.*

The best known inn was *The Mother Red Cap*, a place at one time notorious for its associations with the " Mother Damnable " of Kentish Town. It was here that Moll Cutpurse, the highwaywoman of Oliver Cromwell's days, took up her lodging. Numerous accounts have been given of this shrew, who, it is said, could inspire terror. " The old, ill-favoured creature would at such times lean out of her hatch door with a grotesque red cap on her head. She had a large, broad nose, heavy, shaggy eyebrows, sunken eyes and lank and leathern cheeks ; her forehead wrinkled, her mouth wide and her looks sullen and unmoved. On her shoulders was thrown a dark grey striped frieze with black patches, which looked at a distance like flying bats. Suddenly she would let her huge black cat jump upon the hatch by her side, when the mob instantly retreated from a superstitious dread of the double foe." At one time it was proposed that " the criminals capitally convicted at the Old Bailey shall in future be executed at the cross-roads near the Mother Red Cap Inn, the half-way house to Hampstead." The tavern came into prominence as a public resort about a century since. *The Castle Inn, The Assembly Rooms*, and *The Bull and Gate* have their modern successors in Kentish Town, but there is little trace of rurality in this once-famed hamlet.

Proceeding northward from *The Angel* along High Street, Islington, we encounter many Georgian houses which were remarked upon by coach passengers of other days, for this was the main way out of London to the north. Up to the fourteenth century the old way to Barnet and St.

FIG. 142. DICKENS' CHAIR, THE BOOT, CROMER STREET, KING'S CROSS.

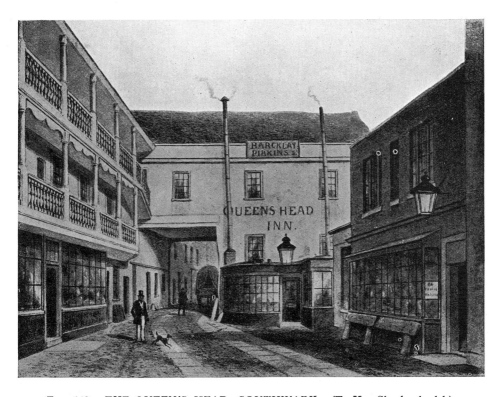

FIG. 143. THE QUEEN'S HEAD, SOUTHWARK. (T. H. Shepherd, del.)

FIG. 144. THE KITCHEN, THE OXFORD ARMS, WARWICK LANE.
(v. also Fig. 42.)

FIG. 145. IN THE OLD SHADES TAVERN, THAMES STREET.

FIG. 146. WAGGON ADVERTISEMENT, STILL IN POSITION AT ELY.
EARLY XIXTH CENTURY.

FIG. 147. "THE FOLLY," ON THE THAMES.

Fig. 148.

"THE OLD GREEN DRAGON." A STUDY OF A GALLERIED LONDON INN.

Albans from London practically ran on the site of the present York Road, missing Highgate Hill and passing through Crouch End. In 1386, the Bishop of London consented to allow a new road to be carried through his park at Highgate. The name Highgate is said to have been derived from the High Gate or Gate on the Hill, there having been the toll gate of the Bishop of London on the summit. The most renowned of the Highgate inns was *The Gate House*. Prior to the forming of the archway and the new cutting, which was projected to facilitate road traffic to the north, Highgate was one of the busiest villages on the North Road. Thanks to its elevation it has preserved many of its inns and not a few traces of its original tea gardens. When the new road to Finchley was in use the Woodman secured most of the custom, but there were still travellers who preferred to enter London through Highgate Village, and so to the West End by Camden Town. *The Spaniards* inn, *Jack Straw's Castle* (Fig. 156), *The Bull and Bush*, recently, alas, rebuilt, and *The Flask* at Hampstead are all so well known, and have been so fully described, that it would be superfluous to do more than refer to them. It is curious, however, that tradition still ordains that Londoners pent within the five mile radius should on occasion follow the footsteps of their ancestors and visit these taverns. There are even some enthusiasts who make a point of leaving the heart of the city on purpose to lunch at the Spaniards. The legend that the steeple of Hanslope church in Northamptonshire can be viewed from the Spaniards has long since been disproved. The author of the story— perhaps it was Mr. Staples—forgot the existence of the five ridges between Hampstead and the Northamptonshire village, and could not have heard of Dunstable Downs. On the other roads out of London will be seen such old taverns as *The Chandos Arms* at Edgware (p. 60), the inns of Waltham Cross and Enfield, the taverns on that section of the Newmarket Road that leaves London at Walthamstow and runs through Woodford and Loughton by the Wakes Arms to Epping. Or, again, evidence of old-time customs can be seen on the eastern road to Romford, Brentwood, Chelmsford, Witham and Ipswich. There are also the old taverns of the Lea Valley, such as the Ferry Boat at Tottenham, and the down-river inns of Barking and the Kentish and Essex shores of the Thames. The southern taverns must not be forgotten. We have already dealt with the famous inns of Southwark; we have mentioned *The Bricklayers' Arms*. The first of this series is *The Horns* at Kennington, which was a stopping place for drivers and carriers from early times. It is not recorded that the ceremony of " swearing on the

horns " was performed here.   At Rye Lane there is an old tavern called
The Kentish Drovers, and until 1830 there was the picturesque *Rosemary
Branch*.   There are but few old inns at Greenwich in these days,
although *The Ship* is fast becoming an antique ; it was an " hotel " a
few years since.   It is for the passing of taverns like *The Crown and
Sceptre* that we lament.   There was a narrow lane leading into Ship
Street, with its swinging signs and gabled fronts forming a picturesque
contrast to the classical dignity of the Hospital, and many other haunts
typical of this nautical quarter of London.   Other South London
taverns include *The Old Crown Inn*, Dulwich, *The Plough*, Lordship Lane,
and *Grove Cottage* at Bew's Corner.   And so, having skirted London
in a wide circle, we can cross the Thames at Kew and reach Chiswick
and Hammersmith.   On this western road from London there are still
signs that tell of the former abundance of small inns and taverns, although
the original character of these houses has changed.   *The Bell and
Anchor*, and *The Red Cow*, were both at one time patronised by travellers
on horseback or passengers travelling slowly by stage-waggon.   The
river front of Hammersmith, from the Eyot at Chiswick to the bridge,
could show a few years since its special type of alehouses, but these are
rapidly becoming scarcer.   Barnes, Mortlake and Richmond have
managed to preserve some of their ancient taverns.   But the lower
road to Richmond was never of coaching importance, and the inns on
this score must be regarded as village concerns.   It is not a little sad
that London has not a range of waterside alehouses in place of the
warehouses of Thames Street and Wapping.   Here and there we chance
upon a merchant's office sandwiched between gaunt masses of brickwork
rising sheer from the water, but such instances are the exception.   In
Wapping such riverside taverns as *The Prospect of Whitby*, *The Turk's
Head* and *The Town of Ramsgate*, back on to the Thames.   At one
time the latter house was known as *The Red Cow*, and it was here that
the fugitive Jefferies was recognised and taken to the Tower.   Farther
down the river is *The Grapes*, in Limehouse Reach (Fig. 138), a tavern
which Dickens renamed as *The Six Jolly Fellowship Porters*, in *Our
Mutual Friend*.

When the Thames could boast only a single bridge, and before
the watermen complained of the unfair competition of the hackney-
coaches, the river was a recognised highway between London and
Westminster, with landing places on both sides.   Little is known of
the riverside taverns of those days, but they evidently existed and
were very popular.   There is evidence in Strype's edition of Stow of

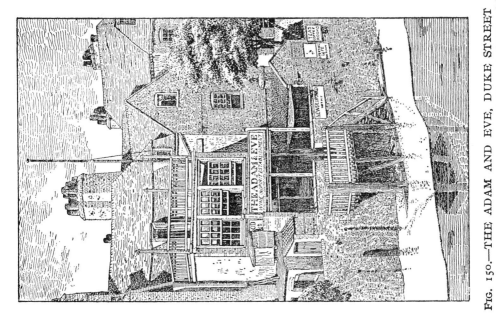

FIG. 150.—THE ADAM AND EVE, DUKE STREET

J. Tavenor-Perry, del.

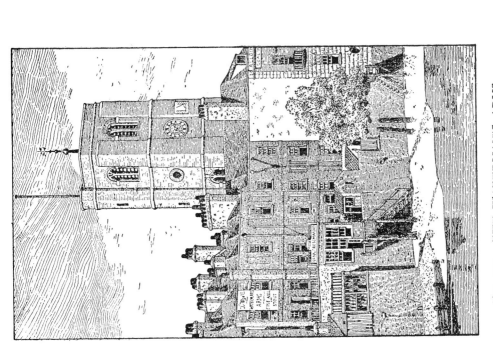

FIG. 149.—THE WATERMAN'S ARMS,
LOMBARD STREET

TWO LONDON RIVER-SIDE INNS.

a curious floating coffee house anchored off old Somerset House. This is said to have been " as bulky as a man-of-war." In the days of Addison and Steele it was a lounge of the wits, and an appendage to the coffee and chocolate houses of Covent Garden and other parts

FIG. 151.—THE BULL, ALDGATE

of the town. In general appearance it looked like the houseboat of to-day (see Fig. 147). It was divided into rooms, and had a platform and balustrade on top. At first it was respectably conducted, and Queen Mary, with some of her following, once visited it. A song of

Fig. 153. THE YARD OF THE GOLDEN CROSS, CHARING CROSS, ABOUT 1830. (G. Scharf, del.)

Fig. 152. THE WHITE HART, BISHOPSGATE.

FIG. 154. THE OLD GEORGE, TOWER HILL.

FIG. 155. THE BULL, ALDERSGATE. (T. H. Shepherd, del.)

FIG. 156.   TEA GARDENS, JACK STRAW'S CASTLE, HAMPSTEAD.
(G. Scharf, del.   *Circa* 1830.)

FIG. 157.   AN XVIIITH CENTURY SKITTLE ALLEY.

FIG. 158. A XVITH CENTURY VINE CARVED BEAM,
STILL IN POSITION IN FLEET STREET.

FIG. 159. THE EAGLE TAVERN AND COFFEE HOUSE, NEAR SOMERSET
HOUSE.

FIG. 160.—THE THREE NUNS, ALDGATE

FIG. 161.—THE SARACEN'S HEAD, ALDGATE

the early eighteenth century, called " A Touch of the Time," alludes
to the Folly :

> " When drapers' smugg'd apprentices
> With exchange girls most jolly,
> After shop was shut, and all
> Could sail up to the Folly."

It was inevitable that *The Folly* should appeal to Pepys, who visited
it on more than one occasion. It was described at a later day as a
piece of whimsical architecture designed for a musical summer-house
for the entertainment of the quality.   At last the place became notorious
and had to be closed.   It was eventually towed away and chopped
up for firewood.

It will be apparent from the material set forth in this chapter
that London and its environs has managed in some extraordinary way
to preserve many examples of once-famous inns and taverns. It is
true that those which have vanished outnumber the survivals ; even
on the roads out of town is this the case, but such as are extant enable
us to reconstruct the past with some regard for truth. A century
since, the inns along the roads in all directions from London were
definite halting places.   There were certain inns used by one line of
stage-coaches and avoided by the opposition.   There were recognised
taverns and inns for stage-waggons to call at, and smaller establishments
for drovers.   There were the taverns with tea gardens in the suburbs
(Fig. 156), catering especially for the London tradesman and his family.
The riverside inns on the banks of the Lea and up-river were frequented
by fishing parties, and the village inns and alehouses off the track
subsisted wholly on local custom.   It would make an interesting study
to trace out the genealogical tree of the inns of the late eighteenth
century and their connection with the Metropolis.   At one time, scheduled
time-tables existed.   Passages could be booked and packages sent in
advance from those inns having business connections with the coach
proprietors.   The mail-coaches represented first class traffic and were
not to be confused with the stage-coaches.   The system was rendered
obsolete by the steam engine.   Within ten years after the opening
of the London and Birmingham Railway the Holyhead road was
practically deserted, and, save for cross-country traffic, the majority
of country inns fell on evil days, and the fine reputation which the
English hostelry had gained for accommodation and good cooking
was shattered.

CHAPTER V

COACHES AND OLD METHODS OF TRAVELLING

IT is not definitely known when the stage-coach first became a feature of English life and travel. Some there are who think that the " short stage," or " hackney coach," marks the first use of a four-wheeled carriage appropriated to the use of the public. These carriages are said to have started from the village of Hackney with passengers for London, and this system of short stage traffic seems to have begun in the reign of Charles I. The early hackney coaches, without windows or springs, were of the crudest description, but the novelty of travelling in them made a great appeal and led to the long distance stage system that was recognised by the end of the Protectorate.

With the Restoration stage-coaches increased in number, and traversed many of the main roads to the chagrin of the tradesmen in and near London, who began to regard the system as a public evil, and voiced their dislike in no uncertain terms and sought to have it abolished. Their attacks were met by counter-statements from the stage-coach owners. One defence of the new order, caused to be published by a stage-coach proprietor, informed the public :—

" Having for the past thirty years established stage-coaches, and since continued them at great risk and expense, the prejudice to His Majesty's subjects in general will be much greater by the putting down of the said coaches than the disadvantage that can be imagined to fall upon any person should the same be continued."

It may seem strange to modern opinion that opposition should have been raised against this early attempt to organise road travel and to make journeys easier, but the same sort of antagonism marked the change from coaching to steam, and from steam to petrol.

Travelling in the seventeenth century has been well described in Fynes Moryson's *Iterinary ; Or Ten Years' Travels Throughout Great Britain and Other Parts of Europe*, published in 1617, and also in a pamphlet entitled, *The Grand Concern of England Explained*, published at the end of the century.

Fynes Moryson, a reliable guide, tells us :—

" In England, towards the south and in the west parts, and from London to Berwick, upon the confines of Scotland, post horses are established at every ten miles, or thereabout, on which travellers ride a false gallop at the rate of ten miles an hour sometimes, but that makes their hire the greater.   With a courier for the chief post-master, or chief Lords of the Council (going either on public business or under the pretence of it) a passenger pays twopence-halfpenny a mile for his horse.   Others who have no such commission must pay threepence a mile."

The second account, written by " A Lover of His Country," declares the running of stage-coaches to be " one of the greatest mischiefs that have happened of late years to the Kingdom, mischievous to the public, destructive to trade, and prejudicial to lands."   In reading his denunciations we must remember that the stage-coaches of 1673 were clumsy and ill-conducted vehicles, and that travelling, with roads in a wretched state, must have been far from a delight.   The writer goes on to say that the stages " engender effeminacy in His Majesty's subjects," who " become weary and listless when they ride a few miles, unwilling to get on horseback, and unable to endure frost, snow or rain, or to lodge in the fields."   He continues :—

" Formerly every man that had occasion to travel many journeys yearly, or to ride up and down, kept horses for himself or servants, and seldom travelled without one or two men ; but now, since every man can have a passage into every place he is to travel unto, or to some place within a few miles thereof, they have ceased to keep horses or to travel with servants."

In the late seventeenth century travel at a speed of three miles an hour was considered to be sufficiently alarming, but when, in the days of Queen Anne and the first of the Georges, this was increased to four miles an hour averaged throughout a long journey, surprise was general.   There are several things, however, which must be considered— the clumsy character of the vehicles, the state of the roads, the irritating delays, and the lack of regular time-tables.

In 1719 we are informed on good authority that the regulations for the post in England are more perfect than those in France ; also that the horses are better.   The coaches, we are told, are of two classes, those that go to all the great towns by moderate journeys, and others called "Flying Coaches," that will travel twenty leagues a day and more, but these do not go to all places.   The sea and the rivers are also used for travelling.   Then there are the waggons, which are great covered-in carts that lumber along, but very heavily, only a few poor old women making use of this type of vehicle.   Defoe, in his *Tour Through Great Britain*, mentions that " Ipswich possesses the advantage of a fast coach that makes London in one day."   Perhaps this was one of the " Flying Coaches."

FIG. 163. THE SALISBURY COACH OVERTURNED AT A STREET FIRE, LONDON. (William Hogarth.)

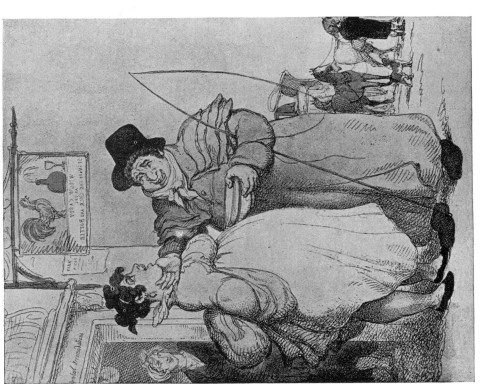

FIG. 162. "A BAIT FOR THE KIDDIES," ON THE GREAT NORTH ROAD. (T. Rowlandson.)

Fig. 164. THE PEDLARS. (J. B. Pyne.)

Fig. 165. THE STAGE COACH IN THE INN YARD. (William Hogarth, sc.)

FIG. 166. THE ROYAL MAIL PASSING A TOLLGATE AT NIGHT. (James Pollard.)

FIG. 167. THE CAMBRIDGE TELEGRAPH AT THE WHITE HORSE, FETTER LANE. (James Pollard.)

FIG. 168. ARRIVAL OF THE STAGE COACH. (James Pollard, 1816.)

FIG. 169. PASSING THE FALCON, WALTHAM CROSS, ABOUT 1833. (James Pollard.)

In the early days of the eighteenth century stage-coaches were not allowed to travel on Sundays, but about 1750 a certain number were licensed so to do. In 1725 the journey from London to Exeter, or *vice versa*, often meant four days on the road. When a Sunday intervened, another day had to be reckoned. In summer the passengers were roused every morning at two o'clock, left the inn at three, and twelve hours later arrived at the end of the day's journey. It will thus be seen that the actual riding time on the road was forty-eight hours. At about ten o'clock in the morning a lengthy halt was made to enable the passengers to dine. This meal was almost invariably a leg (cut) of mutton or a joint of beef, the change being mutton one day and beef the next.

In these early days of coaching the leading horse was ridden by a postillion. By 1740 some stage-coaches began to travel by moonlight, for in *Joseph Andrews* we read that the hero, after being robbed and left for dead by footpads in the night, began to come round as a stage-coach came by. The postillion, hearing a man's groan, stopped his horses and told the coachman. From Hogarth's picture of a *Country Inn Yard* (Fig. 165) we can gather a very exact idea of the coach and passengers at the time of a halt on the road. The scene is an inn on the Dover Road, "The Old Angle Inn, Tom Bates from London," evidently *The Old Angel*, but the locality is not stated.

We will first glance at the passengers. There is a stout lady being assisted out of the body of the vehicle from the top of a flight of portable steps, while an equally stout man watches the manœuvre. There is a diminutive postboy standing near by, attempting to obtain the usual fee. A very corpulent landlady occupies a species of hutch and is engaged in scrutinising the company and ringing a bell. There is a well-dressed man in a heavy travelling cloak disputing the bill with the landlord. On the top of the coach, without any means of holding on, are seated two figures, one a Frenchman, the other an English sailor. In the basket is a woman smoking a pipe, and the exterior of the basket is hung with luggage and packages.

At this period, 1735-1750, stage-coaches were constructed principally of a dull black leather, thickly studded with black broad-headed nails disposed in panels. In some vehicles the upper panels had four oval windows, with heavy wood frames painted red, and sometimes leather curtains. The names of the towns connected by the coaches were painted on the doors. The coaches varied in shape; some were like oval tubs and others were like sedan chairs of overgrown size, the latter the most usual form. The roofs were domed, and, in course of time, were provided with iron guards to prevent outside passengers from rolling off. The coachman and the guard sat on the box seat, which had a heavy hammer-cloth, fringed and ornamented. The guard carried a loaded carbine. Behind the coach was the basket, called in those days the " conveniency." The wheels were of large size and clumsy, as Hogarth's drawing shows, the rims and spokes being painted a bright vermilion. Such machines were generally drawn by three horses, while the progress of the fully loaded vehicle through ruts resembled the labouring of a wooden sailing ship in a heavy sea.

Towards the close of the eighteenth century, roads, coaches and inns were improved. An account of the journey from Dover to London, made on a Sunday in the year 1765, is interesting. The start was made from Dover in two " flying machines," each carrying seven passengers. The journey of twenty-eight leagues was timed to be accomplished in the day, and six horses were attached to each carriage. The fare was one guinea a head ; servants travelled at half-fare in the basket. At each stage the horses were changed and so were the coachmen. This road was notorious for its accidents, and numerous were the complaints and the remedies proposed. There were some who thought that passengers should not be allowed on top, others thought the coaches slung too high, while still others, more enlightened, objected to the curvature of the road surface and the depth of the ruts.

In 1775 coaches usually carried eight passengers inside and ten outside. According to the records there were licensed in that year four hundred road machines and over seventeen thousand four-wheeled carriages. The passing of the Mail Coach Act ruled out many inconveniences, and during the closing years of the eighteenth century there were numerous patents to improve axles, wheels, hubs, and springs. The fashion of travelling on top of the coach eventually came to be considered the privilege of the better sort of passengers, and there was a corresponding increase in charge for outside places. This fashion became popular from the preference of rich people, who rode in the open when using their own carriages. As a result, a change occurred in the order of precedence observed at inns. In the earlier days of travel by road, inside passengers were shown into the best dining-parlour, while the outsiders, who were considered little better than waggon passengers, were directed to the kitchen.

From 1784 until 1840 coaching traffic went through its final phase. Speed and the keeping of time were then regarded of the first importance.

FIG. 170. THE SIGN OF THE BULL, HODDESDON. (J. C. Buckler, del. 1832.)

FIG. 171. WHITECHAPEL TURNPIKE. (T. Rowlandson.)

FIG. 172. THE BATH STEAM CARRIAGE.

FIG. 173. MODERN COACHING: THE KING'S HEAD, HORSHAM.

FIG. 174. DR. SYNTAX STOPPED BY HIGHWAYMEN. (Rowlandson.)

FIG. 175. RESCUE OF DR. SYNTAX BOUND TO A TREE. (Rowlandson.)

Fig. 176. THE START FROM THE INN YARD, EARLY XIXth CENTURY.

FIG. 177. AN AMMONITE AS A MOUNTING STEP.
BRIDPORT, DORSET.

FIG. 178. NOTICE ON GREYS BRIDGE, LONDON ROAD, DORCHESTER.

FIG. 179. HIGHGATE ARCHWAY, EARLY XIXTH CENTURY.

FIG. 180. AN OLD TOLL HOUSE, LYMINGTON, HAMPSHIRE.

FIG. 181. A KITCHEN SCENE, LYMINGTON, HAMPSHIRE   (T. Rowlandson.)

FIG. 182. DR. SYNTAX MISTAKES A PRIVATE HOUSE FOR AN INN.

Fig. 183. DR. SYNTAX ROBBED OF HIS CLOTHES. (Rowlandson.)

Fig. 184. A MAIL COACH SNOW-BOUND. (James Pollard.)

MISHAPS OF TRAVEL, INSIDE AND OUT.

From 1784 night travelling became more general as a means of shortening journeys. De Quincy says : " These mail coaches, as organised by Mr. Palmer, are entitled to a circumstantial notice from myself, having had so large a share in developing the anarchies of my subsequent dreams ; an agency which they accomplished, first through velocity, at that time unprecedented—for they first revealed the glory of motion ; secondly, through grand effects for the eye, between lamp-light and the darkness, upon solitary roads ; thirdly, through animal beauty and power, so often displayed in the class of horses selected for this mail service ; fourthly, through the conscious presence of a central intellect that, in the midst of vast distances—of storms, of darkness, of danger—overruled all obstacles into one steady co-operation to a national result." " Look at those turnpike gates ; with what deferential hurry, with what an obedient start, they fly open at our approach ! (Fig. 166). Look at that long line of carts and carters ahead, audaciously usurping the very crest of the road, ah ! traitors, they do not hear us yet ; but, as soon as the dreadful blast of our horn reaches them with proclamation of our approach, see with what frenzy of trepidation they fly to their horses' heads and deprecate our wrath by the precipitation of their crane neck quarterings ! "

Let us imagine the scene at an inn on the arrival of a coach a hundred and twenty years ago. The coachman has just finished a fast stage ; for the last six miles he has sprung the cattle and has covered the ground on a flat road in twenty-three minutes. He throws down the reins to the hostler, for his work for the time is over. The coach is surrounded by an admiring crowd. Some of the onlookers rush forward to greet their friends and help them with their luggage and bandboxes, others are there to speed departing guests. Within two minutes the fresh team is harnessed, and off goes the coach through the village street, past the idlers and gossips. There are heads at the windows, shopkeepers stand at their doors, old ladies peer from behind dimity screens. Within the smithy the blacksmith pauses to glance at the spanking team, and the guard blows from his " yard of tin " until the village is left and the dust slowly settles. Clear of the houses and the cottages, the guard, having put the horn in the basket, places a pair of brass spectacles on his nose, and, while the coach sways this way and that, affects to read the address on a paper parcel with an air of disdain.

Winter and summer, fair weather and foul, always with a ready word for passengers, always scanning cattle on the road, never failing to notice new tenants in old houses, ready with a smile for schoolboys and a nod to farmers, the guard acts like a demi-god.   He has the latest news from London, the mighty city which so few of the country folk see.   He is the true patron of the inns and the regulator of the time-table.   It is to the guard that most of the passengers defer for information, for none but the privileged dare address the coachman. The guard's life is free and healthy, with hardships in winter, but offering advantages denied to mortals afoot.   Every turn of the road, up hill and down dale, along the valley and between the wooded groves, has something of interest to his all-seeing vision.   He it is who can stop the coach at the cross-roads, and none dare be sparing of a crown tip at the journey's end.

Thanks to the limners, who have left us a legacy of aquatints and engravings, we view the incidents once so real on the great roads of England without leaving the fireside.   We have a view of the early coaches of Hogarth's time (Figs. 163, 165), and from Pollard's drawings (Figs. 39, 166-169) are familiar with the shapes of the crack coaches of the Regency—the " Telegraph " and the " Quicksilver Mail," the " Stamford Regent " and the " York Highflyer " " paper carts "—which, drawn by the pick of teams, made it possible for letters to be delivered to any part of England from the General Post Office within two calendar days.

As we sit in our chairs, we enjoy the whole picture of the coaching era.   We see the roads and the inns, the latter ranking high amongst the architectural treasures of the country.   Some of the inns are picturesque, some are stately, others are quiet and unassuming, but all have that indefinable character which is so essentially insular. We visualise the façades with their ornamental trimmings, we think of the stairways such as those of *The Duke's Head* at King's Lynn and of *The Red Lion* at Truro, and we picture to ourselves the elegant railings of *The George* at Grantham or the balustrade to the staircase within *The Dolphin* at Southampton.   We conjure up memories of stone-paved halls, of wide corridors branching off into labyrinthine passages that have a secrecy of their own, with turns and odd angles, ending in a perfect maze of side issues.

Many of the old inns are still ready to welcome us, and we shall appreciate them tenfold when we are familiar with their story.

Fig. 185.   COTTAGERS' HOSPITALITY TO TRAVELLERS OF A SNOW-BOUND COACH.   (James Pollard.)

FIG. 186.
A XIVth CENTURY INN. (SIGN THE GOLDEN CROSS.)

FIG. 187. COOKING BY CAULDRON AND SPIT BEFORE AN INN, XIVth CENTURY.
(From the MS. Romance of Alexander, Bodleian Library.)

CHAPTER VI

INN SIGNS

THE name of an inn, together with its sign—be that sign displayed on post, board or bracket—can be likened to the name and figurehead of a ship, that is to say of ships that once sailed the salt seas, for save in a few instances the figurehead is no longer met with.

Old signs, as well as good new ones, exercise a spell upon the imagination. When we begin to enquire into their origin, though many articles have been written upon them from the time of Addison, and many others have set out to put all the old signs on paper, we find it still remains for some industrious collector to make a hobby of this pursuit. A modern Johnson, with a company of assistants at his beck and call, might manage it in the span of a quarter of a century. Jacob Larwood and John Camden Hotten truly did much conjointly, but that was in the days when photography was in its infancy, and travel, apart from the railroads, was denied to all except pedestrians keen enough to explore the deserted highways.

There are few in the land unable to read or write, but that is no reason why the signboard should be abolished. It is instinctive to appreciate symbolism. To eye a definite shape, concise and pleasant, is a relief from the written legend. This explains the keen interest aroused to-day by old signs that serve as guides to the status of a tavern. Where a bold and decorative sign exists there will good accommodation be found. It used to be the cleanliness of the mustard pot that constituted a sure index to the quality of an inn and its service ; nowadays the state of a sign is even more trustworthy evidence of the landlord's care for his house and his guests.

By our travels on the roads we are gaining an inner knowledge of commonplace things ; we are learning to respect the work of the craftsman to whom the once-prosperous innkeepers entrusted the task of expressing *The George, The White Hart,* or *The Bald-Faced Stag.* As in most things worldly, the state of business determined the richness or simplicity of the sign. There were also other considera-

tions connected with trade, for inns did not exist for the convenience
of any particular class, but were meant to house those whose regular
comings and goings were an essential part of life's routine.

As we revisit the ancient scenes we are astonished at the variety
of designs as well as the nomenclature. We appreciate the skill of
the blacksmith who thought out the scheme of the scrolls and the
wrought-iron supports (Figs. 187, 192, 197, 207-9). We enjoy the
ingenuity of the carpenter who had such odd tricks of mouldings and
such skill in carving. We wonder at the imagination of the painter
who dared to set his works in the open for all and sundry to criticise.

The majority of signs fall under one or another of the following
categories, or under a combination of two or three of them. They are
historic, heraldic, humorous, prophetic, religious, threatening, appealing,
warlike, peaceful, nautical, amorous, pagan or ecclesiastical. Every
known idea has been drawn upon, for it has been, and still is, the
unwritten code of devisers of signs to woo novelty, and, at the same
time, to hit upon some sort of moral in their contexts. A minor history
of England could be written from inn signs.

We can assume that signs began in the days of Thebes. The
Greeks doubtless had their signs. But we do know of a certainty that
there were streets in Imperial Rome that took their names from the signs
of wineshops, particularly when the bush, the lion or the pig formed
the symbols. The Roman bush of evergreen, which was common to
wineshops, survived the fall of Rome, and, in time, became an accepted
mark throughout Europe (Fig. 7). Thus we can account for its
appearance on the old tapestries and in manuscripts. As one writer
puts it, there may have been the sign of The Cross for Christians (Figs.
186, 187) and Suns and Moons for pagans

Details of tavern customs during Saxon and Danish times in
England are obscure. We may conjecture that weapons might have
been put up to attract warriors, and symbols of agriculture or trade
to attract the hind and the artificer. It is necessary to refer to the
later Middle Ages for heraldic devices, such as crests, shields, coats-
of-arms and escutcheons, as well as the legendary signs that denoted
the proximity of royal forests. Another pleasant thought attaches
to the display of heraldic devices on the walls of noblemen's houses,
who considered it their privilege to protect travellers. Perhaps this
led to a general acceptance of the conventional lion gules or azure,
meaning red lion or blue lion. From this the idea of the rebus was
obtained, such as the bolt piercing the tun, for Bolton, changed in

time to Bolt and Tun ; or, again, an hare and a bottle, for Harbottle. The Crusaders, perhaps, favoured the Trip to Jerusalem, Saracen's Head, the Fleur-de-Lys or the Turk's Head. In time the animal kingdom supplied names, from the camel to the elephant, and the feathered tribe from the eagle to the hawk. Next, attention was directed to vegetables. Later we come to portraits of kings and famous men, views of castles, ships, griffins and dragons, angels, saints and devils.

Gradually the artificers of signs included the painter, the carver, the blacksmith and the mason. For the large inns in mediæval days,

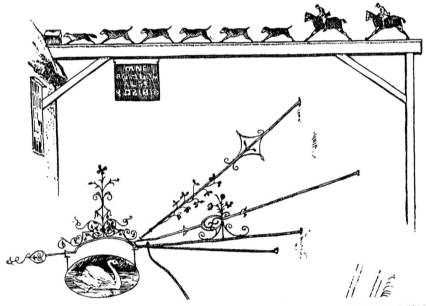

FIG. 188.—THE FOX AND HOUNDS, BARLEY, HERTS, AND THE SWAN, KNOWLE, WARWICKSHIRE (v. also FIG. 273).

such as *The Angel* at Grantham (Fig. 13) and the George at Glastonbury (Fig. 57) a stone corbel formed part of the building, and on it was placed the wooden post that carried the painted effigy of the angel or saint. Sometimes the sign was suspended from a gibbet structure of timber that spanned the street. There is an interesting survival of this type of gibbet at *The George* at Stamford (Figs. 103 and 104), and at Waltham Cross can be seen the Four Swans negotiating the beam (Fig. 68). At Barley, in Hertfordshire, a fox chase is in progress (Fig. 188). From

old drawings we know that the ornate sign of the White Hart Inn at
Scole was once suspended in this way (Fig. 189).

It is pleasant to look through the plays of Shakespeare and the
records of Stow for the names of inns, but it is to London we turn to
verify our range of nomenclature. An ingenious observer in the reign
of James I compiled a document of all the inns and taverns on the
line of route between Charing Cross and the Tower of London. In
Charles I's reign Taylor, the Water Poet, collected the names of the
principal inns of London, and he followed this task by collecting a list
of the tavern and alehouse signs in ten shires and counties about London,
proof that such matters were worthy of notice. Reference can also
be made to the black-letter tract called " Newes from Bartholomew
Fayre " :—

> " *There has been great sale and utterance of Wine,*
> *Besides Beer, Ale and Hippocrass fine,*
> *In every Country, Region and Nation,*
> *Chiefly at Billingsgate, at the Salutation ;*
> *And Boreshead near London Stone,*
> *The Swan at Dowgate, a tavern well Knowne ;*
> *The Mitre in Cheap, and the Bullhead,*
> *And many like places that make noses red ;*
> *The Boreshead in Old Fish Street, Three Cranes in the Vintree,*
> *And now of late, Saint Martin's in the Sentree ;*
> *The Windmill in Lothbury, the Ship at the Exchange,*
> *King's Head in New Fish Street, where Roysters do range ;*
> *The Mermaid in Cornhill, Red Lion in the Strand,*
> *Three Tuns in Newgate Market, in Old Fish Street the Swan."*

From early days innkeepers were compelled to display a sign ;
there are Acts of Parliament from the days of Richard II to those of
Henry VI with definite rulings on the matter, and the withdrawal of
a licence implied the taking away of the sign. During the Great Fire
the majority of old London signs were swept away. They were replaced
by signs of small size in the form of carved stone panels, painted and gilt,
such as *The Swan with Two Necks* in Cheapside. The surveyors at
this period, when the city was rebuilding, seem to have countenanced
new projecting signs of enormous size, but a new Act was passed ordering
that " in all the streets no signboard should hang across, but that the
sign shall be fixed against the balcony, or some convenient part of the
side of the house."

At the opening of the eighteenth century the signs then in being can be summarised from a doggerel verse printed in the *British Apollo* :

> " *I'm amazed at the Signs*
> *As I pass through the Town*
> *To see the odd mixture ;*
> *A Magpie and Crown,*
> *The Whale and the Crow,*
> *The Razor and Hen,*
> *The Leg and Seven Stars,*
> *The Axe and the Bottle,*
> *The Tun and the Lute,*
> *The Eagle and Child,*
> *The Shovel and Boot.*"

It will be gathered from the simple nomenclature which held good for signs at the beginning of the seventeenth century, that ideas current a hundred years later concerned combinations of dissimilar objects ; a change brought about by a confused idea of the meaning of the older signs which were shown without a legend, or by a misconception of French or Latin titles. There is the well-known sign of *The Bull and Mouth* (Fig. 195), derived from the mouth of Boulogne Harbour, and other etymological inexactitudes will suggest themselves. The *Spectator*, No. 28, for April the 2nd, 1710, suggests the appointment of an officer whose duty it shall be to inspect signs and to check absurdities hung out upon the signposts of the City :—

" For want of such an officer, there's nothing like sound literature and good sense to be met with in those Objects that are everywhere thrusting themselves out to the Eye and endeavouring to become visible. Our streets are filled with blue Boars, black Swans, and red Lions : not to mention flying Pigs, and Hogs in Armour.

" My first Task, therefore, should be, like that of Hercules, to clear the City from Monsters. In the second place I would forbid the creatures of jarring and incongruous Natures should be joined together in the same sign : such as the Bell and the Neat's-Tongue, the Dog and the Gridiron. The Fox and Goose may be supposed to have met, but what has the Fox and the Seven Stars to do together ? And when did the Lamb and the Dolphin ever meet, except upon a signpost ? As for the Cat and Fiddle, there is a connexion in it, and therefore I do not intend that anything I have said should affect it.

" As for the Bell-Savage, which is the sign of a Savage Man standing by a Bell, I was formerly very much puzzled upon the Conceit of it, till I accidentally fell into the reading of an old Romance translated out of the French ; which gives an Account of a very beautiful Woman who was found in a Wilderness, and is called in the French la belle Sauvage : and is everywhere translated by our countrymen the Bell-Savage."

At various times in the eighteenth century articles were contributed to the magazines on the subject of sign painters, on the unceasing corruption of names and the growing complexity; for, as the century matured, so it became customary for inn and tavern keepers to appropriate any sign or legend, irrespective of trade or locality, wherewith to deck their particular house. But by this time the sign was no longer functioning in its old and time-honoured capacity, but was fast becoming a purely decorative adjunct to a building.   M. Grisley, a Frenchman who travelled through England in 1765, observes, when he landed at Dover : " I saw nothing remarkable but the enormous size of the public-house signs, the ridiculous magnificence of the ornaments with which they are over-charged, the height of a sort of triumphal arches that support them, and most of which cross the streets."

It is evident, therefore, that in some quarters the old signs of London and other cities were regarded as a nuisance both for their barbarous paintings, ornate designs and ridiculous nomenclature.   Nor were the citizens immune from danger, for more frequently than not the fixings were far from secure.

Not only was the sign the object of attack on the part of numerous critics who looked down upon trade and advertisement, but it began to appear in topographical prints and attracted the attention of Hogarth, who, in several of his paintings, has rendered a very accurate idea of the average inn sign as it appeared to Londoners during the first half of the eighteenth century (as in Fig. 199).   Bonnell Thornton, the editor of the *Connoisseur* in the year 1762, in order to burlesque the exhibitions of the Society of Artists, got up an Exhibition of Signboards. From this time onward legislation seems to have been directed to deter the erection of signs that would be a danger to the public, for in November of the same year the Corporation of Westminster directed " The signs in Duke's Court, St. Martin's Lane, were all to be taken down and affixed to the front of the houses."   This example was followed by other parishes, and the Corporation of London also took action.   Not only the sign-boards but the signposts, too, began to be cleared, until by the time Malton was preparing his aquatints the principal streets were com-paratively clear. The removing of the posts, and the paving of the streets with Scotch granite gave rise to the following epigram :—

> " *The Scottish new pavement well deserves our praise ;*
> *To the Scotch we're obliged, too, for mending our ways ;*
> *But this we can never forgive, for they say*
> *As that they have taken our posts all away.*"

Although, so far as London was concerned, the third quarter of the eighteenth century saw the streets comparatively bare of projecting signs, the tradition for signs was so strong that the signs continued in use but were now afifxed to the house fronts. In the country, however, signs and sign-posts were not interfered with and, as the illustrations in this work show, they have lasted to the present day with many new ones of doubtful taste.

At the beginning of the nineteenth century, when the road and fast travelling became popular, as was to be expected, the signs took on direct allusions to horses, waggons, coaches, and naval and military victories. Reference to old songs and ballads of the seventeenth and eighteenth centuries proves the signs of inns to have been a popular theme. There is one belonging to the days just previous to Waterloo, about one of the last ballads written to celebrate the inn and tavern signs :—

" THE MAIL COACH GUARD "

" *At each inn on the road I a welcome could find :—*
At the Fleece I'd my skin full of ale ;
The Two Jolly Brewers were just to my mind,
At the Dolphin I drank like a whale.
Tom Tun at the Hogshead sold pretty good stuff ;
They'd capital flipp at the Boar ;
And when at the Angel I'd tippled enough,
I went to the Devil for more.
Then I'd always a sweetheart so snug at the Car ;
At the Rose I'd a lily so white ;
Few planets could equal sweet Nan at the Star,
No eyes ever twinkled so bright.
I've had many a hug at the sign of the Bear,
In the Sun courted morning and noon ;
And when night put an end to my happiness there,
I'd a sweet little girl in the Moon.
To sweethearts and ale I at length bid adieu,
Of wedlock to set up the sign,
Hand in Hand the good woman I look for in you,
And the Horns I hope ne'er will be mine.
Once guard to the mail, I'm now guard to the fair ;
But though my commission's laid down,
Yet while the King's Arms I'm permitted to bear,
Like a Lion I'll fight for the Crown."

By the year 1820, coaching and inn-keeping reached the height of prosperity, hence is found the reason for such signs as the *Coach and Horses, The Quicksilver Mail, The Telegraph, The Comet,* and *The Regent.*

George III in effigy gave place to the rubicund features of George IV, and later to the chubby portrait of the Sailor King. Finally, when the faint clank of the locomotive echoed down through the country from Stockton and Darlington, and the London and Birmingham line astonished the countryside, we find such signs as *The Live and Let Live*, *The Railway Swan*, and *The Locomotive Inn*, marking the change and proving to a disquieted world that the roads and inns were about to be neglected. Industry was now entering into its domain and, in consequence, publicans were not slow to encourage artisan customers. Thus we find *Bricklayer's Arms*, *Gardener's Arms*, *Railway Arms*, and a host of Paragons, Railway, Enterprises, and other houses too numerous to index. And so the truth becomes apparent that at all stages the inn signs faithfully record the doings of the time. The painted sign has always attracted the artist, now to draw it for its own sake, now to be commissioned by the publican to paint a new sign and, as not infrequently happened, to pay for board and lodging by finishing up the portrait of a king or the gaudy colouring of a strange monster.

In the late eighteenth and early nineteenth centuries the production of signs was a recognised industry, the chief centre being Harp Alley, Shoe Lane, where it was possible to purchase bunches of gilded grapes, sugar loaves, carved lions, busts, canisters and teapots. In all parts of the country relics from Harp Alley are still to be encountered, sometimes suspended from wrought-iron signs made by local smiths, and at others, as in the case of the Sugar Loaf at Dunstable, standing above the cornice of the portico.

The coach builders and makers of sedan chairs were frequently called upon to paint signboards. It is on record that Cipriani painted a Turk's head, that Samuel Wale, R.A., painted a Falstaff and a full length Shakespeare. Robert Dalton, keeper of the pictures to George III, served his apprenticeship to a sign and coach painter, as well as Ralph Kirby, Thomas Wright of Liverpool, and Smirke the painter. The representation of Admiral Vernon's ship, painted by Peter Monamy, known as the Portobello, was well-known in the first half of the eighteenth century. Hogarth's Man Loaded with Mischief (Fig. 201) is one of the most famous of signs painted by a leading artist. Richard Wilson, it is said, painted the Three Loggerheads for an inn in North Wales, and from this sign the village of Loggerhead nearby would take its name.

We now come to George Morland, who knew the roads and inns of the late eighteenth century more thoroughly than the most energetic

FIG. 189. THE WHITE HART, SCOLE, NORFOLK, 1655. (v. also Figs. 80, 81, 94.) (The sign has now disappeared.) (C. J. Richardson, del., 1825.)

Fig. 190. SIGNS IN DARTFORD HIGH STREET, KENT. (J. M. W. Turner, del.)

traveller. He is credited with *The Goat in' Boots* that at one time graced an alehouse on the Fulham Road, the White Lion for an inn at Paddington, and the sign of *The Cricketers* for a small public house near Chelsea Bridge. Now we understand Morland's habitual carelessness in money matters it is likely that this master more than once left a freshly-painted sign in lieu of payment for the score. His favourite amusement seems to have been to stand in front of the inn doors at Highgate and solemnly to acknowledge the salutes of coachmen and postillions driving through the village in and out of London. Search among the inns at Highgate, however, does not reveal any of his work. To add to the list we have the names of David Cox, of the elder Crome, of Harlow, Sir Charles Ross, Heming, and lastly Millais, who produced a St. George and Dragon with grapes around it for *The Vidlers Inn* at Hayes, Kent.

Lately, there has been a revival of activity amongst artists in this connection, due, no doubt, to renewed interest on the part of innkeepers and the public. There is, for example, an excellent modern sign at the Forest Inn, Hexworthy, representing the inn in miniature. There is a spirited St. George slaying the Dragon at Eaton Socon on the Great North Road, a charming representation of a waggon and horses on the small inn at the crest of Ridge Hill on Watling Street, and the signs respectively of *The Fighting Cocks* and *Postboys* at St. Albans, during the past ten years, have been repainted by Mr. William Webster Hoare, an octogenarian who took part in the Port Darwin expedition of 1864. It is interesting to note, in the case of this amateur sign-painter, that he once sate at the feet of Joseph Nash. Referring again to modern signs, the King's Head, the subject of a wrought-iron sign at Thornham, in Norfolk, the work of a talented craftsman, Mr. Ames, is worthy of study. We have often thought, in our travels on the road, of forming a collection of names of signs with thumbnail sketches of the type of sign and support, but the number threatened to overwhelm all else, so the attempt has been temporarily set aside.

While on this subject, mention must be made of the origin of names and titles, as well as the corruption that has crept in during the course of centuries. Some of the titles are absurd enough. For instance, it is a little difficult to understand the relation of a Magpie to a Crown, a Whale with a Crow, or a Hen with a Razor. The sign of the Leg and Seven Stars is a derivation from the League of Seven Stars, or seven united provinces, the Axe and Bottle being a corruption of Battle-Axe. The Tun and Lute may arise from the association of wine and music, or else be a play on the name of the town of Luton, in Bedfordshire. *The Swan with Two Necks* must originally have been *The Swan with Two Nicks*, the marking adopted for royal birds. The sign of the Goat and Compasses is a corruption of the Puritan sign " God encompasseth us." In like manner, *The Catherine Wheel* became *The Cart and the Wheel*. Regarding the sign of *The Chequers*, this is supposed to have been derived from the armorial bearings of the Earl of Arundel, who in the days of Queen Mary had a grant for licensing public houses, but other authorities state the sign of the Chequers to have been in common use amongst the Romans. George Selwyn could never understand how antiquarians could be at any loss to discover why draughts were an appropriate emblem for drinking houses. The sign of *The Five Alls*, as at Marlborough (Fig. 210), and formerly in Rosemary Lane, London, held the following :—

A King : " I rule all."

A Parson : " I pray for all."

A Soldier : " I fight for all."

A Lawyer : " I plead for all."

John Bull : " I pay for all." Though the persons are occasionally varied in number and effect.

This is a late rendering of an old theme. A hundred years ago the landlord, whose name was Coffin, owned and drove a coach that made a daily journey to London. In his day one of the five parts was a coffin, the inference being that such receptacles held all. The inn at Wantage has a sign consisting of an immense pair of shears.
The Bull and Mouth, previously mentioned, evidently refers to the Mouth of Boulogne Harbour. From the famous inn of that name many of the important coaches started for the provinces. It functioned in those days much as a main line terminus functions to-day. *The Cock* (Fig. 194), the ancient emblem of France, found acceptance as a sign in England because of the allusion to cock-fighting. The Grey-hound (Fig. 196) recalled the royal hunt. The Horse, under various colours, justly signified the means of transport. *The Golden Cross*, Charing Cross (Fig. 153), was also famous for its service of coaches, mostly those on the Chester and Holyhead road, and, at a later date, those from Manchester and Liverpool. The sign of the Flying Horse may have had reference to the messengers of Elizabeth's day who rode

post on the main roads ; other authorities think it to have been derived from early attempts to represent Pegasus, for, as the old song has it,

" If with water you fill up your glasses,
You'll never write anything wise,
For wine is the horse of Parnassus
Which hurries a bard to the skies."

The sign of St. Dunstan is usually associated with the trick played by this saint on the devil.

The Crown and Anchor being the name originally given to a tavern in the parish of St. Clement Danes, the second part of the title may

FIG. 191.—THE COCK, HADLEIGH, SUFFOLK

Basil Oliver, del.

have been taken from the emblem of the anchor which belongs to the legend of St. Clement. *The Devil Tavern* originally stood near Temple Bar. This was a favourite resort of Ben Jonson and had for its sign the Devil, with St. Dunstan tweaking him by the nose with a pair of hot tongs. The house continued prosperous down to the days of Dr. Johnson.

Perhaps by way of compliment and inducement to seafaring men, such signs as *The Mariner, The Jolly Sailor, The Mariner's Compass,* Ships, Boats and Barges have always been favourites in seaport towns. Other signs in this connection include those with the names of victorious admirals, commodores and captains. The Admiral Drake is well known, and here is a comment on Queen Elizabeth and Drake :—

> " *O Nature, to old England still*
> *Continue these mistakes,*
> *Still give us for our Kings such Queens,*
> *And for our Dux such Drakes.*"

The Dog and Duck is the sign formerly adopted for inns frequented by those devoted to the cruel sport of duck-hunting, while the Catherine Wheel commemorates the martyrdom of Catherine, a Virgin and Martyr,

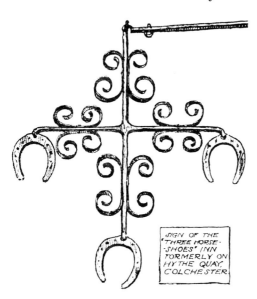

SIGN OF THE 'THREE HORSE-SHOES' INN FORMERLY ON HYTHE QUAY, COLCHESTER

FIG. 192.—THE THREE HORSESHOES, COLCHESTER

Basil Oliver, del.

who suffered at Alexandria in 305 A.D. for her conversion to Christianity. The King's Head, at various times, has been a favourite, except during the Protectorate. *The Robin Hood* refers to the exploits of the celebrated outlaw.

The Cross Inn refers, as can be expected, to the emblem of Christianity and the Crusades.

Regarding the King's Arms a wag once compiled the following explanation, which may well refer to any of the Kings of old, perhaps more particularly to Henry VIII and Charles II : " A certain amorous King holding dalliance with a fair damsel at a public Court ball, one of the courtiers, wishing to retire to some tavern for refreshment, enquired of another what house he would recommend. The reply came pat, ' That he had better not go to the King's Arms, as they were full, but that the King's Head was empty.' "

The Devil and the Bag of Nails is a sign dating from the middle of the eighteenth century. It was probably a satyr with attendant bacchanals, the satyr being taken for the devil and by transmutation the bacchanals were called " bag o' nails." *The Mitre* is a sign of ancient lineage and has invariably been associated with inns that were the

FIG. 193. A SIGN OF THE SUN.

FIG. 194. THE COCK, FLEET STREET.

FIG. 195. THE BULL AND MOUTH. (v. also Fig. 141.)

FIG. 196. GREYHOUND SIGN, CANNON STREET. (J. W. Archer, del.)

FIG. 197. THE SWAN, HARLESTON, NORFOLK.

Fig. 198. SIGNS AT CHELMSFORD —THE ASSIZE PROCESSION, 1762.

Fig. 199. CANVASSING FOR VOTES, SHOWING TEMPORARY ELECTION SIGN.
(William Hogarth.)

Fig. 201. THE SIGN OF THE " MAN LOADED WITH
MISCHIEF." (William Hogarth.)

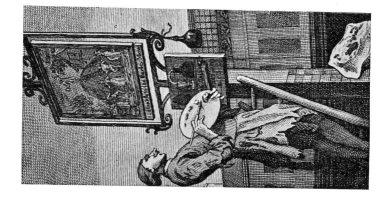

Fig. 200.
THE SIGN PAINTER AT WORK.
(William Hogarth.)

property of church or college. The famous Mitre at Oxford was one of the chief inns bearing this sign. *The Royal Oak* commemorates the concealment of Charles II in an oak tree after the battle of Worcester. *The Mermaid* is one of the ancient signs, and its adoption for the sign

of an inn can be traced back to the fourteenth century. In London, in former times, the Mermaid in Cornhill was the most renowned. There was a Mermaid Inn in Rochester and a Mermaid at Rye, in Sussex (Fig. 59). The Lion is a very general sign and one dating from the twelfth century. It is a national emblem, and there are, of course, variations, such as black, blue, red, gold and white. We have never heard of a brown or grey lion.

The Fortune of War is a title dating from the first half of the eighteenth century, and possibly has some connection with the winning of prize money by the landlord, a returned soldier or sailor. There was formerly a *Fortune of War* in Giltspur Street, London. The Wrestlers is a sign found in various parts of England, probably alluding to the once popular sport of

FIG. 202.—THE WHITE HART, BLETCHINGLEY, SURREY (v. FIG. 27)

W. Curtis Green, A.R.A., del.

wrestling. The original eighteenth century wrought-iron standard to *The Wrestlers* at Highgate, on the right side of the Great North Road at the crest of the hill, is still to be seen. One authority is of the opinion that the sign of The Wrestlers commemorates the bout between Francis I and Henry VIII on the Field of the Cloth of Gold. The Nell Gwynne appears to have been just adopted during the popularity of the King's favourite. The Black Bell: In the days of Stow there was an inn called the Black Bell nearly opposite to the spot where the Monument now stands. It was a large

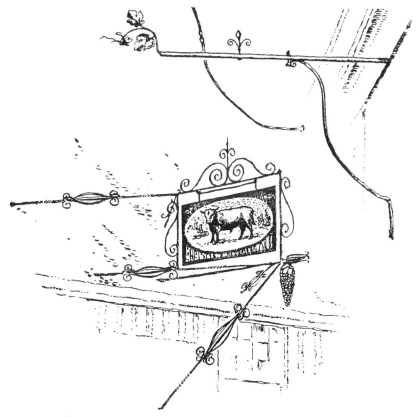

FIG. 203.—AT CLARE AND SUDBURY, SUFFOLK

Sidney R. Jones, del.

house of stone, at one time the residence of the Black Prince. *The Crown Inn* was at the east end of Crown Field, an open space in Cheapside about the middle of the thirteenth century. This emblem of royalty has been freely used in all parts of the country. *The Saracen's Head*, a famous coaching inn, was at Snow Hill, whence certain stage-coaches departed for the north. There is a Saracen's Head, now the

Pomfret Arms, at Towcester (Fig. 86). The inn at Snow Hill, it is said, took its name from the fact that the mother of St. Thomas à Becket was a Saracen, but probably it had its origin in the Crusades. *The Angel*, a title like that of the Mitre, refers to church-owned hostelries. The Pope's Head was at one time a complimentary sign, and later on a derogatory one. The World Turned Upside Down was the name of a public-house on the road to Greenwich. It represented the globe with a man walking on the lower part of it. *The Magpie and Crown* is a curious corruption. It is said that originally the sign of the Magpie was the only name for the particular inn at Aldgate referred to ; later it was changed to the Crown, but the business not prospering the Magpie was brought back to keep an eye on the Crown. *The Magpie and Stump* is an unmeaning title derived from the picture of a magpie seated on a branch. *The Marquis of Granby* was a favourite sign for inns in the latter part of the eighteenth century. It was intended as a compliment to the Marquis of Granby who flourished between 1721 and 1770. *The London Prentice* was the name of an inn formerly in Old Street, near to Shoreditch church. Chaucer says :—

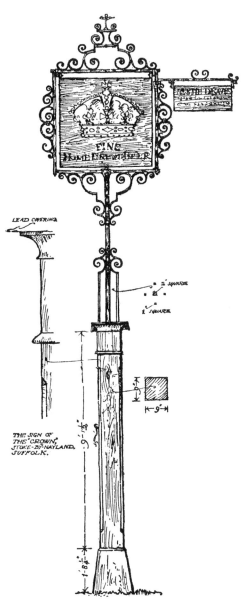

" *A prentice wilom dwelt in our citee*
   At every bridale would he sing and
      hoppe, [*shoppe.*"
He loved bet a taverne than the

FIG. 204.—THE CROWN, STOKE-BY-NAYLAND, SUFFOLK.

Basil Oliver, del.

The Nag's Head Tavern was the name of an old inn formerly in the Borough, frequented by carriers from Kent.   It was, and is, also the name of a tavern in the Holloway Road, London, and one time an ale-house on the way north and east.   *The Punchbowl* was formerly a small tavern, since rebuilt, on the Watling Street, near the twenty-third mile stone from London.   This, and *The Botell, The Tun* and *The*

FIG. 205.—THE BULL, BRUTON, SOMERSET;

E. Guy Dawber, del.

Barrel, are appropriate signs for inns.   Various combinations of these signs will suggest themselves.   *The Hat* was the sign of a tavern frequented by hat-makers.   It may also bear some reference to the Cardinal's hat.   *The Feathers* and *The Plume of Feathers* are signs that refer to the Prince of Wales.   There is the famous *Feathers* at Chester, and another at Ludlow (Figs. 89, 92, 93, 96), and *The Plume of Feathers* at Princetown, on Dartmoor (Fig. 126).   *The Hat and Feathers* is a

FIG. 206. THE WHITE HART, DORCHESTER.

FIG. 207. AT BUNTINGFORD, HERTFORDSHIRE.

Fig. 208. THE SWAN, MARKET HARBOROUGH.

Fig. 209.   THE BULL, REDBOURN, HERTS.   (*v. also Fig.* 107.)

Fig. 210.   THE FIVE ALLS, MARLBOROUGH.

Fig. 212. THE WHITE HART, GRETTON, NORTHANTS.

Fig. 211. A DISMANTLED SIGN FORMERLY AT THE FOUNTAIN, BEDFORD.

Fig. 215.   THE GLOBE, SAWTRY.
(v. also Fig. 242.)

Fig. 214.
THE KING'S ARMS, CHRISTCHURCH.

Fig. 213.
AT WOODSTOCK, OXFORDSHIRE.

FIG. 216.   AN XVIIITH CENTURY TRADE CARD IN THE FORM OF AN
ORNAMENTAL WROUGHT IRON SIGN.

FIG. 217.   THE BLACK BULL, WATLINGTON, OXFORDSHIRE.

FIGS. 218, 219, 220. TYPICAL INN TRADE CARDS. (The top subject was drawn and engraved by Hogarth, and re-engraved a century later for the same inn.)

Figs. 221, 222, 223, TRADE CARDS OF THE SWAN
WITH TWO NECKS, LAD LANE, LONDON.

combination of the previous titles. *The Hat and Tun* was an inn at one time near Hatton Garden, and may have a primary reference to the family of the Hattons.

The Horns Tavern is a name that refers to inns frequented by cattle drivers from the shires conducting cattle to Smithfield (see previous remarks on meaning of the horns at Highgate). The Horns at Kennington is well known. It is also likely to have some reference to the chase. Shakespeare makes frequent references to the veneration of the horns as a crest. *The Boar's Head* figured as the sign of several inns; the most noted is the one immortalised by Shakespeare, which was situated in Eastcheap. The Virgins, like the Angel and the Mitre, denotes church ownership. *The White Hart* was a favourite sign for taverns in the Middle Ages, and is found in all parts of the country. There is a White Hart at Dorchester where the effigy stands over the inn door (Fig. 206). There is also the famous White Hart at St. Albans, dating from the fourteenth century, where Hogarth painted the portrait of Lord Lovat a few days previous to the execution on Tower Hill. There are White Harts at Salisbury, at Waltham, in Essex, at Ampthill, in Bedfordshire, and, in fact, near to every former royal demesne. Edwards refers to the number of White Harts in East Anglia.

The Half Moon Tavern was formerly the name of an inn in Aldersgate Street. There is an alehouse of this name at Stoke Climsland, in Cornwall, dating from 1760. The Fox was a common sign in country towns and villages. *The Fox and Grapes* refers to the fable. The Old Parr's Head refers to the longevity of Old Parr. It was adopted as the title of a sign to an inn in Aldersgate Street. Under the portrait of the ancient gentleman was painted the following :—

> " *Your head cool*
> *Your feet warm,*
> *But a glass of good gin*
> *Will do you no harm.*"

Butler's Head was named after the author of *Hudibras*. Chalk Farm was the tavern notorious for ducks, and later as a tea-garden on the Hampstead Road, near Primrose Hill. *Baptist Head* was the name of an inn at one time in Aldermanbury, adopted, it is thought, at the time of the Commonwealth, in allusion to St. John.

The Cherry Tree was the name of an inn formerly in Bowling Green Lane, Clerkenwell, noted for its garden of cherry trees. The Lamb refers to the Church and to the Crusades, and later came to have an agricultural significance. *The Plough, The Harrow, Barley Mow, Hayrick, Wheat-sheaf, Ploughman, Ploughboy, Jolly Farmer, Waggon and Horses*, all have a farming significance. *The Antelope*, like the title of the White Hart, refers to the royal pursuit of hunting.

The Bush (Fig. 7) was a sign used from the earliest times, in common with the Grapes, to let all and sundry know, whether they could read or not, that good liquor could be had within. Johnny Gilpin was a sign borrowed from Cowper's humorous poem. The Bear and Ragged Staff was a title taken from a part of the armorial bearings of the Earl of Warwick. *The Hand and Shears* was the title of an old sign formerly in Cloth Fair, Smithfield. *The May Pole* refers to May Day customs. The last maypole in London was in the Strand. As Pope says :

> " Amidst the area wide they took their stand
> Where the tall maypole once o'erlooked the Strand."

Alestakes were formerly confounded with maypoles.

The George and Blue Boar in all probability refers to royalty hunting the wild boar. There is no reason for the wild boar being described as blue. It was the name of the important inn in Holborn whence, at the beginning of the nineteenth century, many of the west-bound coaches started, and where condemned criminals had a drink on their way to Tyburn, some promising to pay on their way back. *George Inn* undoubtedly bears reference to St. George, and later, to the four Georges who ruled England. Like *The King's Head, King's Arms*, etc., it had some reference to loyalty on the part of the innkeepers and their customers. The George Inn, in the Borough High Street, of which only a fragment remains, was the starting point for many Kent, Surrey and Sussex coaches. It was also a centre for stage-waggons which went out of London with goods and returned with hops. It is on record that London porter was made exclusively from Kentish hops.

The Ship Inn was a sign common to nautical towns, although it is frequently met with in the heart of the country. The Ship at Reading is well known. There is the Ship at Dover, a once noted house for travellers to and from the Continent. The sign was generally painted to represent *The Great Harry*, a three-decker, a frigate or a brig. The Pitt's Head refers to both the elder and younger Pitt. *The Goose and Gridiron*, probably suggested by *The Swan and Harp*, is a sign whose origin is one of those curious fantasies common to eighteenth century houses. There was at one time an inn of this name on the north side of St. Paul's Churchyard, which was a sort of terminus for short-stage coaches drawn by three horses, making the journey to Hammersmith, Brentford, Hounslow, Ealing, Kew and Richmond. *The Grave Maurice*: this sign refers to the naval exploits of Prince Rupert, who lost his life in a hurricane. *The Horse Shoe, Three Horseshoes*, etc., bear no historical evidence of being set up for the benefit of farriers. Such signs may have arisen from the superstition that a horsehoe is a lucky possession in trade. *The Ship and Shovel* was the title of an alehouse near to Dagenham Beach, in Essex. *The Golden Bull* was a sign of great antiquity, and is said to date from the time of the Emperor Constantine, who was presented by his British soldiers with a golden bull. *The Eagle and Child* is part of a crest of the Stanleys, the family of the Earls of Derby, and in part reveals the legend of the illegitimate child found at the foot of a tree on which an eagle had built a nest. The crest was afterwards altered by a descendant of the family to an eagle preying on a child. *The Bull Inn* at Whitechapel, in the eighteenth century, was the resort of the Essex farmers who journeyed to London once a week to sell produce. One of the landlords, a man named Johnson, was formerly " boots " at this inn. *The Sun* was a sign probably of pagan origin. It is a favourite tavern sign (Fig. 193). In the eighteenth century the symbol of the Sun was further decorated with the legend beneath, " The best ale sold here under the Sun."

Brace Tavern was the name of an inn kept by two brothers of the name of Partridge, hence the title. *The Bell*, Old, New, *The Ring of Bells, Five Bells, Eight Bells, Peal o' Bells*, nearly all allude to famous church bells in the vicinity. *Castle and Falcon* was the name of an inn formerly standing near Aldersgate. *The Thatched House* Inn was the name of an inn at Hoddesdon immortalised by Izaak Walton. *The Thatched House Tavern* was the famous meeting place of the Architects' Club, from whence sprang the Royal Institute of British Architects. *The Moonrakers*: This title for some reason appears to have been associated with Wiltshiremen. *The Rose Tavern* was a sign common to all parts of England. It refers to the Wars of the Roses, and, later, in Tudor times, the title became the double-barrelled one of Rose and Crown.

No part of an ancient inn is more subject to change and the toll of the weather than the sign, be it fixed or swinging, of iron, copper, wood or painted canvas stretched on wood. Hence it is that in museums,

and among the lumber which still exists and repays enquiry in out of
the way places, it is rare to chance upon inn-signs, wooden effigies, or
ordinary paintings earlier in date than the close of the seventeenth
century.   The carved Angel over the entry to the Angel and Royal
at Grantham is an exception.

Of wrought-iron signs of late seventeenth century date there are
many weather-worn examples.   The aspect of Chelmsford in the early
part of the eighteenth century, as seen in old prints (Fig. 198), to some
extent recalls the character of many London thoroughfares of contemporary date.   In this print will be seen divers manners of signs ;
some swing as though from a gallows, others are bracketed from the
wall with sundry stay-bars and supports, and others are placed flat
against the wall.   One of the finest wrought-iron signs, dating from
1700, enriches the white-stuccoed front of *The Swan* at Market Harborough (Fig. 208).   The fabric of this house is of greater antiquity
than the façade.   The wrought-iron sign of the Swan is of exceptional
interest, for it shows strange fancies, evidently the work of an artist
craftsman of ability, who designed a grille which has a silhouette somewhat
like a bracket-clock.   In this there is a painted swan.   There are
supporting swans as subsidiary features to make the scheme more telling.
Perhaps subconsciously the craftsman was a humorist and wished to
express all the attributes of this attractive hostelry.   The sign of the
Swan at Harleston (Fig. 197) is of early eighteenth century date.   This
small oval sign is triangulated on a decorated bracket from a brick
front.   The ironwork, together with that of the projecting balcony
below, gives increased richness to the façade.

Two other signs of the same period are illustrated.   One from *The
White Hart* at Gretton, in Northamptonshire (Fig. 212), and the other
from *The Bull Inn* at Redbourne, in Hertfordshire (Fig. 209).   The
latter is of the hood or sheepshead type, and in this shows sympathy
with the design often adopted for long-case and bracket clocks.   The
triumphal arch or gibbet form of sign, such as the example which at
one time functioned to the inn at Scole, is now rarely seen.   There
is one of this type at Stamford (Figs. 103 and 104), another to *The Four
Swans* at Waltham Cross (Fig. 68) ; yet another at Barley (Fig. 188),
illustrating a fox chase, and a simpler one at Longstreet on Salisbury
Plain.

Apart from being novelties, such signs as the foregoing give
increased perspective to a street, for they frame in a medley of different
groups of roof, chimney-stack, doorways and odd projections.   Such

signs in the past were decorative adjuncts to the streets of Chelmsford and Dartford (Figs. 190 and 198), and they imparted something of a triumphal progress to the volume of stage coaches that passed beneath them. John Gilpin could not have paid much attention to the sign at Hoddesdon when he clattered through.

Other inn signs of the late eighteenth and early nineteenth centuries are of the single post type with wrought-iron hood, within which swung the sign-board. There are good examples of this type at *The Bear* at Woodstock (Fig. 213), the King's Arms at Melksham, and *The King's Arms* at Christchurch (Fig. 214). Most signs of the central support type stand on the opposite side of the road to the hostelry, in some cases they are arranged on the same side of the way, with wooden drinking troughs for cattle. The inn called *The Anglers* at Bell Weir has a wooden sign attached to the wall representing a party of anglers feasting in the open. An interesting wrought-iron sign is that of *The Three Horseshoes* at Great Mongeham, bearing the date 1735; there is another at Colchester (Fig. 188). *The Windmill* at Tabley, in Cheshire, is a painted sign representing Don Quixote tilting at the windmill. *The Smoker* at Plumbley, in Cheshire, shows the famous racehorse " Smoker " with the jockey. *The Beehive* at Grantham is a real skip on the top of a post with an active swarm of bees. On a swinging board, projecting from the post, is painted " Stop, Traveller,"

> This wondrous sign explore,
> And say when thou hast viewed o'er and o'er
> Grantham, now two rarities of thine
> A lofty steeple and a living sign."

Two other forms of signs connected with road travel must be mentioned. The first is the façade of a farrier's at Carlton-on-Trent, on the North Road, where the front shows an immense horseshoe with nails complete in brickwork. The second is the interesting legend, painted on the wall of the coach-builder's shop at Ely, referring to road transport to *The Bull Inn* at Bishopsgate Street (Fig. 146).

Those who are interested in past customs should study old walls and yards of inns. They will find many legends and notices which have survived. Some of these signs refer to the sale of wine and beer, to tobacco, and the names of landlords and landladies long forgotten. Other signs are directional and give the distances from the inn to points on the main road, as well as from London. There are the old bell-boards, on which can still be seen names of the principal apartments

and the numbers of the bedrooms.   All such are usually fine examples
of the signwriter's skill in lettering.   We would also include those
legends which give the name of the inn so obtrusively across the whole
façade, for they are eloquent of the tendency which crept in during
early railway days for coaching proprietors to cut out stops, therefore
the landlord had recourse to large-type appeals designed to catch the
eye of outsiders.   Happy are travellers to-day if, in their enquiries,
they chance upon the gauze blinds of old inns with their lettered legends,
some of which, as at Lymington, in Hampshire, tell all and sundry
that copies of the *Shipping Gazette* can be seen within.   There are,
too, the painted boards giving the time-table of the express coaches,
those famous turnouts which issued forth from the Bull and Mouth
and careered all the way to Holyhead.

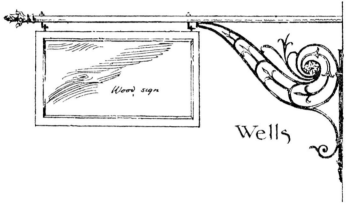

ORNAMENTAL IRON BRACKET BEARING INN SIGN

CHAPTER VII

SMALL INNS, ALEHOUSES, WAYSIDE TAVERNS

In London the once famous coaching houses have become merged with modern buildings, but a different aspect of the subject is presented when the smaller tavern is studied. We have found it convenient to turn to the provincial cities and country towns to study the subject in its more special bearings, and so we find it similarly convenient to adopt the same point of view for smaller examples of old places of entertainment. Every country town has its bevy of tumbledown drinking places which, by some strange chance, are still prosperous. They stand at odd corners, or they are buried amidst a network of houses, in pothouse confusion forming a class by themselves. In the old days of road travel, no coach or stage-waggon honoured these houses, few of which had adequate stable accommodation, but on market days they formed, and still form, centres to which drift certain elements of the countryside population. At Waltham Abbey, little more than thirty years ago, the market place could boast a row of such small taverns. Gradually the licences were withdrawn, and now there are three only, where formerly ten or twelve competed. St. Albans (Fig. 224) offers another example of a country town with a superfluity of taverns attendant on the larger hostelries. But sordid as some of these taverns are, to all outward appearance, some at least have architectural merit, and the interest from the point of view of local tradition and custom is increased by the *bonhomie* of the clientèle. In mediæval times, and, indeed, down to the beginning of the nineteenth century, before Telford improved the roads from London to Holyhead, one of the ways from London made its entry into St. Albans at a point about half-way down Holywell Hill, as though the objective had been the Abbey Tower. At the southern corner of this road is a long house of fifteenth century construction, sadly altered externally, but retaining traces of having been an important inn in the fifteenth, sixteenth and seventeenth centuries. Within this house is a large kitchen which has

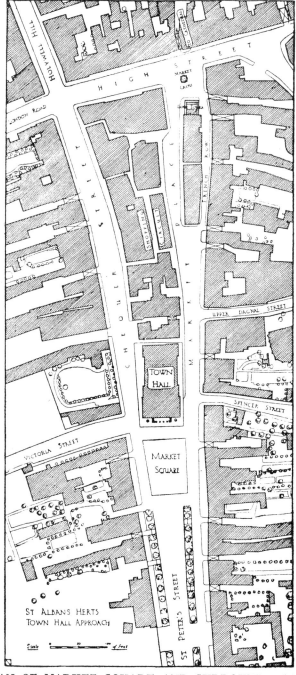

FIG. 224.—PLAN OF MARKET SQUARE AND SURROUNDINGS, ST. ALBANS

the distinction of holding its original stone fireplace.   The road traveller who wishes for first-hand information as to the uses to which this tavern has descended, has but to open the door, when he is confronted with a scene which causes him to think that time has stood still.   It is that of a tramps' kitchen, the temporary abode of all who are journeying between London and the Midlands on foot, and have not the where-withal to pay for more expensive lodgings.   All sorts of meals are being cooked at the fire, the company for the most part are true wayfarers, with as many coats as backs, and they travel light, scorning the casual ward, independent of work, eager for the morrow with the unexpected, a confraternity of men who have no ability to concentrate but whose chief interest is to wander.   One wonders at the particular view of life such travellers have.   They are fairly happy and contented—that goes without saying—they are care free and have no fears of rent, rates or taxes.   They are friendly-disposed, and jest with the officers of police who look in, and, moreover, they have no jealousy for the enquiring stranger who plies them with questions if he bids so fair as to offer them a pint.   Is it not a little strange that the mendicants who thronged at the gates of the Abbey, centuries since, should have representatives of their order on the same spot in this enlightened age ? True is the saying, " the world affords not such inns as England hath." We have said that the small inn is a thing apart from the lordly tavern, and it is a fact that the same hospitable spirit pervades all classes of inns.   There is *The Fountain* at Canterbury, which is reputed to have accommodated the wife of Earl Godwin in 1029, and later lodged the murderers of St. Thomas à Becket.   We have mentioned the Ostrich at Colnbrook (Figs. 70, 73), and now take the opportunity to state that it was once the scene of a number of murders which made the Bath Road notorious.   Many small taverns claim to date from the fifteenth century, and there were monastic inns, pilgrim inns, and church inns.

The Star at Alfriston (Fig. 65) belonged to the Abbey of Battle, and there were numerous others on the pilgrim ways and the routes taken by mariners crossing the country from port to port.   In the England of the past, the tavern and the alehouse were part of social life.   We tell of their function by the names on the signs.   At Wendover, in the street that leads through the town, across the Chilterns from the Thames Valley to Dunstable, there are several small taverns, including *The Nag's Head* and *The Pack Horse*, which show this route to have been a pack horse track.

Sidney R. Jones, del.

FIG. 225.—THE UNION, FLYFORD FLAVEL, WORCESTERSHIRE

There are many with the name of *Pheasant, Dog and Gun,* and *Fox and Hounds,* as well as *Horse and Groom,* to tell of sporting proclivities. The small tavern and the alehouse, therefore, bring us face to face with not the least of the varied interests of the road. There are the small inns which have the merit of recording historical events. Charles the First slept at the George at Burford, and decided to surrender to the Scots at the Saracen's Head at Southwell. At *The Crown* just outside Uxbridge, now known as the Old Treaty House, he began the conference with the Parliamentary Party.

Nearly every minor alehouse has its legends and traditions of highwaymen such as Turpin and Duval, with many other high Tobymen who have earned a place in the national biography of crime. There are the inns of lonely heaths (Fig. 263), the riverside inns (Figs. 110, 111, 127, 227), and the inns of the south and west country where Exciseman Gill and his following were wont to pursue the contrabandists.

The smaller and less inviting inn has a charm for the curious which is undeniable. There is always the chance of a discovery of some rare antique. Chance one day took the authors of this work to *The King's Arms* at Bicton, in Devonshire, where they found a company of landworkers regaling themselves with cider. One of the farm labourers stole out and returned with a model in earthenware of a cow which, he said, was at least three hundred years old. He showed no resentment when it was pointed out to be Wedgwood of the late eighteenth century. On another occasion, at Colley Weston, the landlord, who could find nothing in the larder, eventually produced a fine plum cake which he declared was made according to a recipe prepared by his great grandmother, and this, with gin toddy, made an excellent meal.

In the late eighteenth century it was George Morland who found delight in the subject of the alehouse (Fig. 228), a theme that suited his lust for wandering and the conviviality of drinking companions below his station. The following paintings of this type by him may be mentioned : " The First of September," " The Dram," and " Evening." The second, " The Dram," shows a picture of the " Black Horse," evidently a scene in Hertfordshire.

Another shows a scene on the Exeter Road, where the driver of the London and Exeter stage waggon is persuading a country girl to accompany him to London. What a picture of old English life the versatile Rowlandson presents in the " Horse Fair at Southampton," with the group of horsemen before the tavern door. The Woolpack at Hungerford introduces us to road travel, we see a huge stage waggon in full progress drawn by a team of six horses. He shows, too, a view of Broadway with an inn that has long since vanished. There is the scene at Cardiff in which an inn figures. For an authentic view of an inn interior we have " A Soldier's Tale," from the original in the Ashmolean Museum at Oxford (Figs. 181 and 229). There is another called the " *Woolpack Inn*," and a view of Honiton, with the dashing " Exeter Fly," but his best virtues are reserved for the illustrations to " Doctor Syntax " (see Figs. 114, 174, 175, 182, 183).

FIG. 226.—THE MORITT ARMS, GRETA BRIDGE, YORKS

Hugh Mottram, A.R.I.B.A., del.

Although *The George* at Greta Bridge in old days was an important house, it does not rank, in point of size, with some of the better known inns. Charles Dickens immortalised this and the New Inn by combining the names in Nicholas Nickleby. The George Inn has the advantage of a picturesque setting, standing as it does by the stone bridge which carries the North Road across the Greta river. Like many other hostelries from which the glory has departed, the George has been converted into tenements.

FIG. 227. THE FERRY, HORNING. NORFOLK.

FIG. 228. THE ALEHOUSE INTERIOR. (George Morland.)

FIG. 229. AN INN KITCHEN, NEWCASTLE EMLYN, SHOWING DOG IN TURNSPIT.
(T. Rowlandson, about 1800.)

Fig. 230.   THE CAT AND FIDDLE, HINTON ADMIRAL, HAMPSHIRE.

Fig. 231. RECRUITING AT LISKEARD, CORNWALL. (T Rowlandson.)

Fig. 232. "SOLDIERS' RAMBLES" (T. Rowlandson.)

Another famous Dickens tavern is *The King's Head* at Chigwell, which the novelist renamed the Maypole by reason of its Tudor associations. "The Maypole was an old building with more gable ends than a lazy man would care to count on a sunny day ; huge zigzag chimneys, out of which it seemed that even smoke could not but choose to come in more than naturally fantastic shapes imparted to it in its tortuous progress ; and vast stables, gloomy, ruinous and empty. The place was said to have been built in the days of King Henry the Eighth, and there was a legend not only that Queen Elizabeth had slept there one night while on a hunting excursion, in a certain oak-panelled room with a deep bay window, but that next morning, while standing on a mounting-block before the door, with one foot in the stirrup, the Virgin monarch had then and there boxed and cuffed an unlucky page for some neglect of duty."

" With its overhanging stories, drowsy little panes of glass and front bulging out and projecting over the pathway, the old house looked as if it were nodding in its sleep. Indeed, it needed no great stretch of fancy to detect in it other resemblances to humanity. The bricks of which it was built had originally been a deep, dark red, but had grown yellow and discoloured like an old man's skin ; the sturdy timbers had decayed like teeth, and here and there the ivy, like a warm garment to comfort it in its age, wrapt its green leaves closely round the time-worn walls."

While on the subject of the small inn and tavern, mention must be made of the regional characteristics which are usually expressed in the structural features. A typical Surrey inn is *The Old Bell* at Oxted, the timber framing of which dates from the second half of the fifteenth century. This inn underwent alterations in the eighteenth century, and recent alterations in the quasi antique manner have done little to add to its beauty. The old inn, like most of the smaller hostelries of Surrey and Kent, occupies a prominent corner site in the village, not the least of its attractions being the massive timbers, the elegant spur-piece and the flight of stone steps at the side. Here can be seen a tethering post which has done service these hundred years past. Another regional type is *The Crown* at Cheddingfold (Fig. 249).

The Cat and the Fiddle at Hinton Admiral, Hampshire (Fig. 230), is long and low, but its builder contrived to fit two stories within the steep-pitched roof. It is a wayside house typical of the district and belongs to the period of the second half of the eighteenth century, and on that count is related to many of the cottages and farmhouses which adorn the villages of Hampshire from Romsey to Poole.   Such small houses, while well known to lovers of the road, and patronised by local customers, have little claim to notoriety.   Their interest chiefly lies in their domestic character.   If there is one thing about the building of such places, it is the " common touch " exemplifying the traditions of a thousand years which no learning can impose on crude material to-day.   The proportions are diminutive, the timbering almost extravagant in its scantlings, the fireplace in the tap-room seems large enough to accommodate a crowd, while the woodwork of the high-backed settles, no less than the surface of the roughly-plastered walls, indicates a finish by contact, unnoticed and unintentional.

The small inn is a reflection of local life and custom ; hence it is that, while the coaching house has an archæological interest, the alehouse and the tavern convey a more direct idea of the survival of tradition. There is nothing more enjoyable than to take one's ease on one of the rude benches outside an inn of this sort in summer and to gain a view of the comings and goings of the villagers.

In the evening, after the day's work, the field workers come in to chat and all are eager for news.   Then it is that yarns are spun, that jokes are broadcast and scandal slyly discussed, that village fathers become illuminating on political matters.   The alehouse is the village club, there is a *bonhomie* and friendliness among the habitués that would astonish the members of a London club.   The countryman takes his tankard at the inn with a sense of a good day's work behind him, he is a connoisseur in judging malt liquor and his views of particular brews should be cultivated.

Within the tap-room there are the side-shows of shove ha'penny, or shuffle board, of dart throwing, and the mild pastime of bagatelle. The stranger who asks for a tankard is viewed with covert glances by the assembly.   He is generally set down as a foreigner from London. If he ventures to talk to the company, he is a bold man and clever if he gains an audience.   After he has left, he will be discussed from the hair of his head to the cut of his coat.

Every small tavern has one or two curiosities in the shape of Staffordshire china figures or a bottle with a model ship inside.   There are a few of those notices, so common half a century since, dealing with " A Fugitive from Justice named Trust who murdered Credit."   Sometimes one chances upon an old militia notice or a broadsheet advertising local sports of a century earlier.

The chimney corners of alehouses are the most alluring features. At *The White Hart*, Bletchingley, the fireback, and irons and utensils have been grouped for the admiration of those who frequent the inn (Fig. 27). Another good interior is to be seen within *The Red Lion* at Bierton, near Aylesbury, an inn singularly free from faked antique splendour.

In Hertfordshire and Bedfordshire brick and tile predominates in the buildings. *The Blue Boy* at Hertford, which adjoins the Blue Coat School, was built at the time the school was founded. The builder gave the alehouse a distinctive pediment, perhaps as a compliment to learning. *The Hen and Chickens* at Botley presents a fair brick front with the adjoining weatherboarded stabling. It has outside benches, a pair of inquisitive gables and a fine clump of brick forming the central chimney stack.

The Red Lion at Water End, near Gaddesden, is a prim three-storied house with two bay windows, speaking forcibly of the opening years of the last century.

Essex has many small inns constructed of timber and finished externally with weatherboarding. *The Plough and Sail* at Paglesham is representative of the series. No inn could possibly be more aptly named, judging by its outward appearance, than *The Jolly Farmer* at Farnham, Cobbet's birthplace (Fig. 233). *The Plume of Feathers* at Princetown, on Dartmoor (Fig. 126), was built some years before the war prison was opened for French and American prisoners. This is a three-storied house with a weathercoat of slate, which is one of the distinctive features of west country building tradition. *The Leather Bottle* at Cobham, immortalised by Dickens, is too well known to be further described.

On the borders of the Tamar, where the road leaves Devon for Cornwall, there is an interesting stone-built tavern called the Royal, which, in addition to the curiously shaped Gothic windows, has a typical west country porch. While writing of Cornwall, the " *First and Last House*," Lands End, is worthy of remark. At Countess Weir, on the Exe, is an excellent inn built a hundred and twenty years ago. Many of the small inns have a pretension to greatness. For example, *The Waggon and Horses* at Longworth almost ranks as a diminutive coaching-house of the late eighteenth century. In this house, the Georgian front is symmetrical. There are two deep bay windows, twin entrances, and a graceful gambrel roof to unify the three first floor windows. Of the Georgian alehouses we have *The Bell* at Brook, the Eight Bells at Hatfield (Fig. 235), *The Waggon and Horses* at the top of Digswell Hill, and *The Flask* at Highgate.

In London Road, St. Albans, there is to be seen the Peahen Tap which, in the spacious days of coaching, terminated the long range of stabling that fronted the new and improved road to London. At the rear of this house there was a coach-builder's yard, for repairs on the road were then, as now, of vital importance.

A charming interior is forthcoming within the inn at Overton Ferry, St. Ives, in Huntingdonshire,* where the chimney corner is inviting and the shelves populous with brass and china ; the whole assemblage being presided over by an ancient long case timepiece in the corner.

On the cross roads of England many of these interesting survivals of past social life stand invitingly. There is the alehouse called *The Six Lords*, in Buckinghamshire, which may have reference to Stowe. There is *The Folly*, near Towcester, *The Four Crosses*, by Lichfield, *The Flying Horse* at Clophill and *The White Hart* at Maulden.

The ancient market town of Ampthill, in mid-Beds, fifty years since had almost as many inns as large houses. *The Red Lion* in Church Street is now a private house. *The King's Head*, dating from Tudor days when Henry VIII. and Anne Boleyn came to the Royal Honour for hunting, is the headquarters of a territorial regiment. There is *The Rising Sun*, an attractive inn, *The Crown and Sceptre*, with a yard adjoining the brewery, *The White Hart* with its imposing array of sashed windows, and *The King's Arms*. It was from the latter house that the stage-waggon set forth every Thursday and reached *The Windmill* in St. John's Street, Clerkenwell, on the afternoon of the Sunday following. In those days, 1775, the post office formed part of the King's Arms.

We have taken the case of Ampthill and its famous brewery as an example of the enterprise of brewers like the Morris family, who equipped the small inns of the countryside within a radius of a dozen miles. Joseph Morris, the founder of the firm, was a Quaker. He was not only a good brewer, but he had a flair for architecture, and to his influence can be attributed the care expended in constructing many of the inns owned by the firm. The design of *The Compasses* at Clophill is a case in particular. This house was planned and built a century since, and it shows in its material, as in its proportions and detail, how thoroughly good building was understood. As late as 1850, when the firm built

* Illustrated in E. C. Pulbrook's *English Country Life and Work.* 1923.

FIG. 233.   THE JOLLY FARMER, FARNHAM.

FIG. 234.   THE COACH AND HORSES, WIMBORNE, DORSET.

FIG. 235.   A DICKENS INN, THE EIGHT BELLS, HATFIELD.

FIG. 236.   THE ROSE AND CROWN, STANTON, SUFFOLK.

Fig. 237. THE OLD MAYPOLE, RICKMANSWORTH. (Hanslip Fletcher, del.)

Fig. 238. THE SWAN, ELSTOW, BEDFORDSHIRE. (Bunyan's Village.)

FIG. 239. TAPROOM OF A COUNTRY INN, ABOUT 1837. (Thomas Silson, del.)

FIG. 240 FIREPLACE AT THE CASTLE, OLD SARUM, SALISBURY, WITH BAKING OVEN BY INGLENOOK.

FIG. 241. THE WHITE HORSE, SPALDING, LINCOLNSHIRE.

FIG. 242. THE GLOBE, SAWTRY, HUNTS. (*v. also Fig* 215.)

FIG. 244. THE THREE TUNS, TILEHOUSE STREET, HITCHIN

FIG. 243. AN INN YARD, CHALFONT ST. PETER, BUCKINGHAMSHIRE.

Fig. 245. TOTTENHAM HIGH CROSS AND OLD SWAN INN. 1822. (G. Scarf, del.)

FIG. 246. AN EIGHTEENTH CENTURY HARVEST CELEBRATION. (From a Contemporary Print.)

The Chequers on the Bedford Road, it was the boast that Cubitt could not have built it more thoroughly. An interesting history of the enterprise of the country brewers in this connection could be written. And so we come to the present time, when the fashion is to transform every inn that does good trade, to smarten up where smartness is undesirable, and to replace quiet comfort with alarming ostentation. What a number of pseudo-antique inns are being built all over the country without regard to artistic decency! Who would care to quote Herrick within the parlour of one of these modern taverns? —

> *Come sit us by the fire's side;*
> *And roundly drinke we here*
> *Till that we see our cheekes ale-dy'd*
> *And noses tann'd with Beere.*

No account however lengthy would be complete if it did not include some reference to the fishing inn. In the seventeenth century the Londoner, bent on sport, made his way to the upper reaches of the Fleet River, between Hampstead and London, or if he was of more venturous disposition, he hied to the River Lea, taking the road from Shoreditch to Tottenham, Hoddesdon and Ware.

The following are excerpts from the *Compleat Angler.*

THE FIRST DAY.

(A Conference between an Angler, a Falconer and a Hunter, each commending his recreation.)

Piscator, Venator, Auceps.

Piscator : You are well overtaken, Gentlemen! A good morning to you both! I have stretched my legs at Tottenham Hill to overtake you, hoping your business may occasion you towards Ware, whither I am going this fine fresh May morning.

Venator : Sir, I, for my part, shall almost answer your hopes; for my purpose is to drink my morning's draught at the Thatched House in Hoddesdon, and I think not to rest till I come thither, where I have appointed a friend or two to meet me! But for this gentleman that you see with me, I know not how far he intends his journey: he came so lately into my company, that I have scarce had time to ask him the question.

Auceps : Sir, I shall by your favour bear you company as far as

Theobalds, and there leave you; for there I turn up to a friend's house, who mews a Hawk for me, which I now long to see.

. .

(*He leaves the two for Theobalds.*)

Later.

Piscator to Venator : I am glad your patience hath held out so long for we are within sight of the Thatched House. I'll now lead you to an honest Ale-house, where we shall find a cleanly room, lavender in the windows, and twenty ballads stuck about the wall. There my hostess, which I may tell you is both cleanly, and handsome, and civil, hath dressed many a fish for me ; and shall now dress it after my fashion and I warrant it good meat.

ANOTHER OCCASION.

Piscator to Venator (*discussing a great trout*) *:* Ay marry Sir, that was a good fish indeed : if I had had the luck to have taken up that rod, then 'tis twenty to one he should not have broke my line by running to the rod's end as you suffered him. I would have held him within the bent of my rod, unless he had been fellow to the great Trout that is near an ell long which was of such a length and depth, that he had his picture drawn, and is now to be seen at mine host RICKABIES, at the George in Ware.

ANOTHER OCCASION.

Piscator, Peter and Coridon. Peter, and Coridon and I have not had an unpleasant day : and yet we have caught but five trout : for indeed we went to a good honest ale-house, and there we played at Shovel board half the day : all the time that it rained we were there, and as merry as they that fished. Come, hostess, give us more ale, and our supper with what haste you may : and when we have supped, let us have your song, Piscator, and the catch that your scholar promised us : or else Coridon will be dogged.

ANOTHER EXPEDITION.

(*Piscator and Venator walking towards Tottenham.*)

Piscator : And so you are welcome to Tottenham High Cross.

Venator : And pray let's now rest ourselves in this sweet shady arbour, which nature herself has woven with her own fine fingers : 'tis such a contexture of woodbines, sweetbine, jasmine, and myrtle ; and so interwoven as will secure us both from the sun's violent heat, and from the approaching shower. And being set down I will require a part of your courtesies with a bottle of sack, milk, oranges and sugar, which, all put together, make a drink like nectar ; indeed, too good for any but us Anglers.

There are many old fishing inns by the rivers of England.   There is
the inn at Turvey, in Bedfordshire, known by the sign of *The Five Fishes*,
the inn at Great Barford, on the Ouse, and *The Anchor* at Tempsford,
the latter house being one of those curious versions of Tudor architecture
which became fashionable in 1837.   In addition must be mentioned
The Trout at Godstow, on the stripling Thames above Oxford, old-
established and famous (Fig. 265).   Some of the fishing inns have the
sign of the Ship, others are known by *The Jolly Anglers*, *The Fish Inn*,
The Barge Inn, *Angler's Rest*, *The Ferry Boat*.   In addition, there are
Swans, Moor Hens, Whales and Ducks, all of which have a watery
significance.

Ben Jonson knew the alehouses of the villages near London as well
as he knew the Mermaid.   Old Hobson, the courier, must have known
every house and almost every tree between London and Cambridge.
So we pass to the Restoration with Pepys often on the road to Brampton.
There are writings of Defoe to prove the extraordinary attractions
of early eighteenth century inns, especially those he mentions in *Moll
Flanders*.   And so through the eighteenth century we find poets like
Gay and Shenstone, writers like Fielding, Smollett, Sterne, Boswell and
Sheridan, time and again referring to inns and recording impressions.
In the late eighteenth century the inn and the tavern attract the painters
to follow the lead given by Hogarth.   There are the small inns painted
by Morland (Figs. 228 and 256) and Rowlandson (Figs. 229, 231), invaluable records of the common life of the time.   In the early nineteenth
century the joys of the tavern and the inn appear in the songs of the
people, but strange to say few writers, with the exception of Sir Walter
Scott, thought them of moment.   It was left to Charles Dickens to become
the historian of road travel.   The early nineteenth century inn has its
charms, for it is a true reflex of the custom of the day and has a place
as unique in its way as the more picturesque survivals of the Middle
Ages.   The majority of old inns as they stand at the present time
are the result of slow growth and many alterations and additions which
in no wise detract from their character. Many a house started as a
timber-framed structure, and in the ensuing centuries took on successive
veneers of brick and tile, of stucco and weatherboarding.   Any inn
in any part of the country can be taken as a fair example of this process
of adding and altering.   It is not possible to say who planned and built
the inns other than to indulge in the conjecture that the earliest were
built by master builders and workmen who contracted separately
for the several trades.   The Georgian inns, which to a large extent

inherit the earlier traditions of craftsmanship in their fabric, were built by master bricklayers and carpenters.

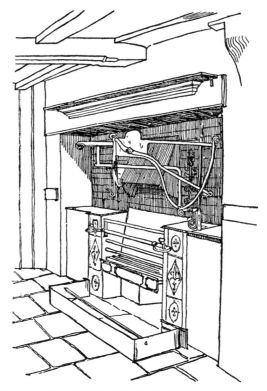

IN THE WHITE HORSE, KERSEY, SUFFOLK

Basil Oliver, del.

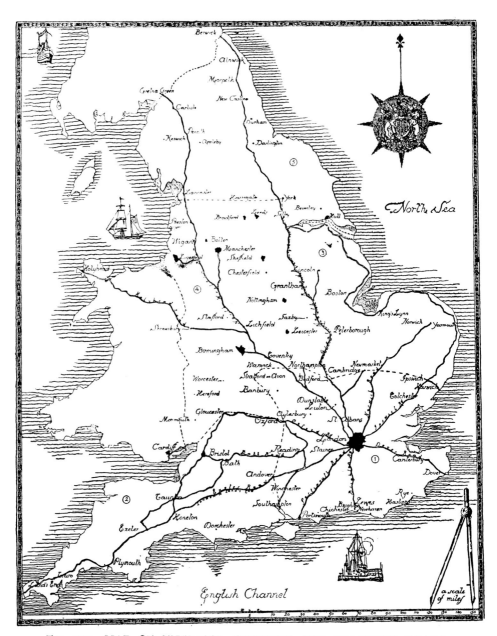

FIG. 247.—MAP OF ENGLAND, SHOWING OLD COACHING ROADS

CHAPTER VIII

TOURING

ENGLAND has many attractions, and not the least is the revelation, by revival of road travel, of unexpected interests along routes infinite in variety, which, during the railroad era, were unfrequented. To plan a tour is the major contribution to its success ; the old-time traveller rarely made a journey without a road book. In the past the roads, the towns, and the inns were as familiar as the railways and the main line junctions are to-day. The modern road book is a sequel to Cary and Paterson, but as the main and cross-country roads have lost their former significance, a brief summary of English topography becomes essential. There is, however, need for something more than an index to the fine old inns. By dividing the country into districts, the basis of a series of tours suited to varying tastes is offered for development.

This work includes numerous pictures, but it is obvious that the scope of the subject cannot be compressed within the pages of a single book. The full number of first-rate inns which still survive on the famous mail-coach routes, as well as in small country towns and seaside resorts, is almost inexhaustible. One of the fascinations of the subject lies in surprise and unexpected discoveries, even among the derelict examples which have been converted into mean tenements or degraded into public-houses. None can claim to have more than a cursory acquaintance with the inns of England, for minor hostelries exist by the hundred, fronting the village green ; some with bucolic bay windows stand in towns, and others are in peaceful by-lanes, awaiting discovery. These inns occasionally rise to a surprisingly good menu, and although the request for a plain tea may be looked at askance and the suggestion of sleeping accommodation often refused, lodgings can be found in the vicinity and difficulties overcome. The interest of an inn is its capacity for entertainment in every sense. There is the delight of encountering antiquity, of viewing the relics of the past, not in museum formation, but still in everyday use. There is the humble inn with its well-worn appointments, the settle, the chimney corner and sanded floor, the pleasant buzz of conversation and the placidity that refuses to be hurried.

Various are the methods to be adopted in planning a tour which has for its objective the study of inns. Happy are those who possess a calf-bound coaching book, an Ogilby or Paterson, with the main routes defined and a list of the principal centres, as well as an appendix of the cross-roads and distances. To follow the course of a trunk road, such as the way to Bath, to Holyhead, or to Edinburgh, the latter either by the East Coast or the even more interesting route through Carlisle, is to enter in spirit into the experiences of those who have used these roads in the past. From selected centres it is possible to range at will from the high roads to the lanes, through towns, villages and hamlets, in the valley and along the hill tops, and thereby gain a picture of the countryside.

To make this method easy the map of England, excluding the Celtic fringe, has been divided into five sections, S.E., S.W., E., W. Midland and N. Reference to the key map shows these divisions, as well as the main trunk routes, while separate maps are given to each of the districts. In the introduction to each of the divisions the geological formation is indicated, for this determines not only the scenery, but the local materials with which the inns are mainly built. Some idea of the villages and a few historical associations are mentioned. Routes can be worked out with convenience by the aid of Bartholomew's half-inch to the mile series of maps, supplemented where greater detail is desired by the sheets of the one-inch ordnance survey, which are to be obtained almost everywhere.

The profession of inn-keeping has gained in status since the revival of road travel, and the tourist can generally rely upon satisfactory accommodation. The choice of hostelry depends upon the taste of the traveller ; there are "5-star" houses and others of more modest pretensions which are recommended by the Automobile Association. Occasionally the tourist must be prepared to encounter shortcomings in regard to meals and accommodation, but such inconveniences are the exception.

Outside the cities and towns almost any rural district has attractions for touring, whether in the home counties, the South West, the heights of the Chilterns or the Cotswolds, the undulating lands of the Eastern Counties, the rich Midland Shires or the broad stretches of the Northern fells.

It is by no means necessary to follow the usual routes or to pursue, with guide book exactitude, the more frequented roads. The chief delight of England is the widespread survival of the unspoiled country. Even

FIG. 248.   A DESTROYED KENTISH INN : THE SIX BELLS, HOLLINGBOURNE, KENT.

Fig. 249. THE CROWN, CHIDDINGFOLD, SURREY.

Fig. 250. THE RED LION, MARTLESHAM, SUFFOLK.

such industrial areas as the Black Country and the collieries have the quality of contrast and come within the picture, but the tourist will turn to the cathedral cities and the county towns for the rich harvest of the unexpected.   To name a few routes where roads are good, scenery delightful and the village inns unspoiled, there is the road from Exeter through Tiverton, Bridgwater and the Cheddar Gorge that misses Bath and proceeds through the Cotswolds to Warwickshire ; there is the route through East Anglia to Norwich which can be traversed clear of towns. There is the route from the Vale of Evesham through Worcester to Malvern and Wrexham, that fringes the Welsh border.   There are the ways of Derbyshire, the coastal roads of Lincolnshire, the Yorkshire Wolds, the byways of Kent and Sussex, and a score of others running between main roads such as the diverging byways from London which in old times were independent means of inter-communication with less important towns.   These lesser roads await the compilation of a modern itinerary for their existence proves them to have been the mediæval ways of local or long-distance inter-communication.   Those showing more direct coach routes are in the category of seventeenth and eighteenth century road travel.   From the point of view of exploring the associations that still cling along the roadside, these routes afford the most pleasant method of enjoying the country.   Much has been done by the Road Board to provide new signs and maps.   It is note-worthy that motorists are discovering their own routes out of London, and avoiding centres of towns and that a new order of road-making is in progress.   For example, it is possible to travel from King's Cross to Highgate free of trams and traffic, to gain the North-Western route by Regent's Park, to travel the first stages from London to Brighton by Chelsea, and through Streatham to Dover, to make for Norwich by the Ferry Boat at Tottenham, and for the West Country by Harrow and Uxbridge.   There is another route from London to the Midlands which in mediæval times was used when the historic Watling Street was in decay ; this runs by Chalk Farm to Hampstead and proceeds to Mill Hill, Arkley, Shenley and St. Albans, thence it bears north-west to Hemel Hempstead, Gaddesden, Leighton Buzzard and avoiding Buckingham eventually leads to Banbury, Stratford and Warwick.

Division I.—S.E. England

To Londoners as well as to tourists, this corner of England has an especial interest for it holds much of the country that has escaped spoliation and at the same time there are roads out of town which avoid

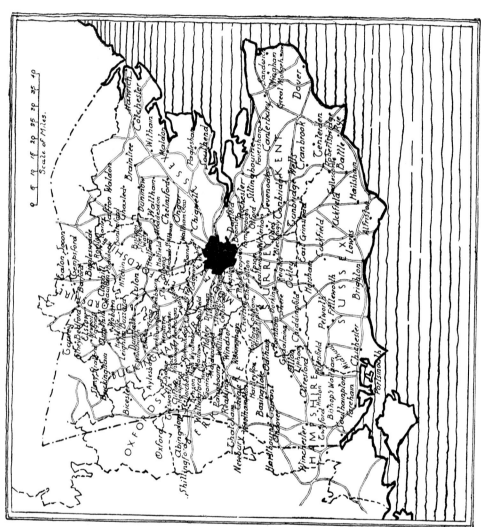

FIG. 251.—MAP OF SOUTH-EASTERN SECTION

suburban and crowded districts. The limits of this division are as follows : On the West, by the series of routes which come in arterial sequence from Warwick through Banbury and Oxford to Newbury, Andover and Southampton ; on the North, by a line from Warwick to Bedford and from thence to Cambridge, Newmarket, Ipswich and Harwich ; on the East, by the coast routes which give access to the ferry at Tilbury and thence across the Thames to the fringe of the S.E. coast. This district is rich and diversified ; it is sub-divided into North and South of London. The centre of this country is the basin of the London clay with a series of chalk heights and ridges which run north-east and south-west to the North of London and in Essex form a range of low divided ridges ; on the north-west the ground rises to the wooded chalk heights of the Chilterns which border the slightly undulating plains beyond. On these heights there are many small inns which have signs recalling the pack horse and the wool-carrying of other times. The Bedford Road, which was the main road to Derby and as such is frequently mentioned in the story of the Pretender and the rising of 1745, particularly those accounts referring to the passage of troops and baggage, formerly ran from London by Barnet and through a series of lanes to St. Albans. Thence it went by Harpenden to Luton, crossing the Icknield Way, and so by Wrest to Elstow and Bedford, Higham Ferrers and Leicester ; it was partly remodelled by Telford. There are at least three routes to the North which come into this section, the oldest is Ermine Street, or the old North Road, which runs from Shore-ditch Church to Ware, Royston, Huntingdon, Alconbury Hill and Stamford. The second route is from Whitechapel to Buntingford and from thence to Newport and Cambridge.

The third, of mediæval origin, is the road over the heights of Highgate to Barnet, Hatfield, Welwyn, Baldock, Buckden and Alconbury Hill. Mention must be made of the important post road which leaves the Great North Road at Welwyn and is continued via Hitchin, Henlow, and other villages to Girtford Bridge, where it rejoins the Great North Road. Of the roads in the north-western direction there is the Edgware Road to St. Albans, formerly Watling Street, which in olden times aimed for the city of Verulamium, the ruins of which lie below St. Albans. Telford, who made the new road from Barnet in 1825, altered its course at various points, but traces of the old road can still be studied, as beyond the chalk cutting at Dunstable. The Colchester Road runs by Brentwood and Chelmsford, having for its objectives Ipswich and Harwich. There are many old towns on these roads and a riband of inns.

By studying the map it is possible to avoid the densely populated Lea Valley and other London suburbs, for in spite of intensive development many parts near London have retained the old character. The hilly routes especially stand up above the bricky surroundings defined and secure. Contrary to usual opinion, Essex will be found to have well-wooded uplands, and its chief flats formed in early times the morasses and sloughs of the Thames estuary. To name a few towns beyond those already given which have retained features of road travel of other days, there are such places as Cheshunt, Elstree, Hoddesdon,

FIG. 252.—WHYMAN'S INN, CASTLE STREET, CAMBRIDGE

W. B. Redfarn, del.

Much Hadham, Witham, Saffron Walden, Thaxted, Shefford, Ampthill, Woburn, Winslow and Potton. Here are to be seen inns of every degree with entries for the hooded stage waggon, archways for coaches formed before the days of outside passengers, and chaste openings neatly bricked to tell us of the " Highflyers " and " Comets." In such towns the intimate social life of the past still lingers, the smithies are in operation and old customs flourish. It is true that the carrier's cart is more rarely seen, its function having been usurped by the local

FIG. 253.   THE WHITE HORSE, BISHOP'S STORTFORD.

FIG. 254.   THE PLOUGH, KINGSTON VALE, BERKSHIRE.

FIG. 255.   THE BELL, HURLEY-ON-THAMES.

FIG. 256.   A MOORLAND ALEHOUSE.
" The Thatcher " (by George Morland).

Fig. 257.   THE ELEPHANT AND CASTLE, BAMPTON, OXFORDSHIRE.

Fig. 258.   A FISHING INN, THE TROUT, GODSTOW, UPPER THAMES.

Fig. 260.   THE WHEATSHEAF, TEWKESBURY.

Fig. 259.
THE SEVEN STARS, ROBERTSBRIDGE, SUSSEX.

motor van or bus ; the saddlers' shops have entered on their last phase, but the decaying interests have yet an appeal in their decline.

South of the Thames the scenery is entirely different for the geological formation is extraordinarily diversified and quite hilly. From the Thames basin the ground rises to the chalky formation of the North Downs, which forms a height east and west, facing due south. The country between is well wooded and undulating, there are extensive views across to the South Downs, a parallel height over the sea with a north facing escarpment running from Dover into Hampshire and Wilts. In this "tumbled valley of the Weald," with its crust of stiff clay and pine-feathered heights by Sevenoaks and Ashdown Forest, will be encountered endless Commons, sandy heaths and the innumerable village greens which go to make the garden of England. In other days the Weald was largely inaccessible. The natural obstacles forbade the making of direct routes, and for long the ribbon-like tentacles of London have been checked. The main routes to the coast are along the lines of least resistance, for example that to Rochester, Chatham, Sittingbourne and Canterbury, with branches to Deal and Dover. There is the central route from Maidstone, which avoids the Pilgrim's Way. There is the Brighton Road with alternate routes which the Royal Charioteer-in-Chief brought into prominence. Then we have the Portsmouth Road, the way through Guildford, Hartley Row, to Winchester and Southampton, with branches through Romsey and the New Forest to Poole and Dorchester. In the south the counties have been little industrialised ; the towns, with the exception of Chatham, have all the distinction they possessed a century ago. One thinks instinctively of the Borough and its old inns (Figs. 133-5, 140, 143) when one is at Canterbury, at Rochester or Maidstone, just as one thinks of the "Commodore Coach" with its complement of officers for Chatham, the Margate Stage, and the fast coach to the "Ship" at Brighton. In addition to these main routes, there are cross roads which enable the tourist to avoid London and to travel from Dover to Warwick and the North, from Southampton to Oxford, and from Brighton, through Horsham to Guildford, Reading and Bristol.

Few things are more delightful than a tour, by whatever method of locomotion is preferred, through the Weald of Kent and Sussex, where pleasant wooded undulating scenery of the quiet English type serves as a background to villages built of local materials, picturesque in grouping, and in their variety of timber construction, tile-hanging, weather-boarding and plaster, with occasional buildings in Georgian brick, flint, or rough ragstone. It is unnecessary to mention more inns individually, for they must be considered as part of the hamlet or small town. Where Kent joins Sussex there is the altogether admirable situation of Goudhurst or Tenterden, and, to take two examples, we can visit *The King's Head* at Sissinghurst, or *The Queen's Head* at

FIG. 261.—THE THREE CROWNS, CAMBRIDGE.

W. B. Redfarn, del., 1875

Sedlescombe. Further east we find the forest country, with such villages as Hartfield or Withyam, and the South Downs rising above the western Rother valley, as at Fittleworth, with its *Swan*, and Midhurst (*Spread Eagle and Angel*), shading into the thatched villages of the Hampshire chalk, as in the upper Bourne Valley near Andover off the Newbury Road, through Hurstbourne or Vernham. The number of village routes is endless, the by-roads are largely of reliable surface and the tourist can explore endlessly.

Amongst smaller towns there are little Westerham, with its winding streets and the mansion of General Wolfe ; Sevenoaks, with its gables and Georgian cornices ; Tonbridge, with its maltings ; Canterbury, with its gates and walls ; Guildford, with its Clock-face ; Horsham, Midhurst, Petworth, Odiham and Alton. One views with relish the good manners of Winchester and the baked brick of Reading. There are such significant features as the windmills of the south-western region, the spinning cowls of the oast-houses, in the cheerful tone of brick interspersed with Kentish ragstone, flint and timber, the old tales of the men of Kent, the journey to the sea, and the inevitable charm of wide-spreading and mysterious distances.

DIVISION II.—SOUTH-WESTERN ENGLAND

A preliminary to discussing this region is to take an approximate line from Oxford to Gloucester, and from thence to Bristol and the coast. On the east the line is defined by the road from Oxford to Southampton ; this division includes Wiltshire, Somerset, Dorset, Devon and Cornwall. The regional characteristics of the buildings vary considerably and are most clearly defined in the simple work of granitic Cornwall. The geological formation of these regions begins with the great chalk boss of Wilts with its attendant clay, the limestone and slate of Somerset with much flat alluvium, the old red sandstone of Devon and the igneous granite rocks of Dartmoor and Cornwall. These materials have influenced local tradition, to which the buildings respond.

From Andover as a centre there are three roads to Exeter and the west ; from Bath there is the road from Glastonbury and Wells to Taunton, as well as the road over the Mendips to Axbridge and Bridgwater ; there is the coast road from Dorchester to Honiton and Exeter, and thence by Dawlish to Plymouth. In Cornwall there are roads to Land's End from Launceston through Truro and Penzance, and that from Tor Point through Liskeard and Bodmin. The cross-roads in Cornwall are narrow and hilly.

The south-western section offers possibilities for rambling tours which cannot fail to yield in every way a remunerative return in tumbled hill scenery, in beautiful villages and picturesque old inns. To start from the finely situated little town of Shaftesbury, with its wide, sweeping view over the Blackmoor Vale, a road winds southward to

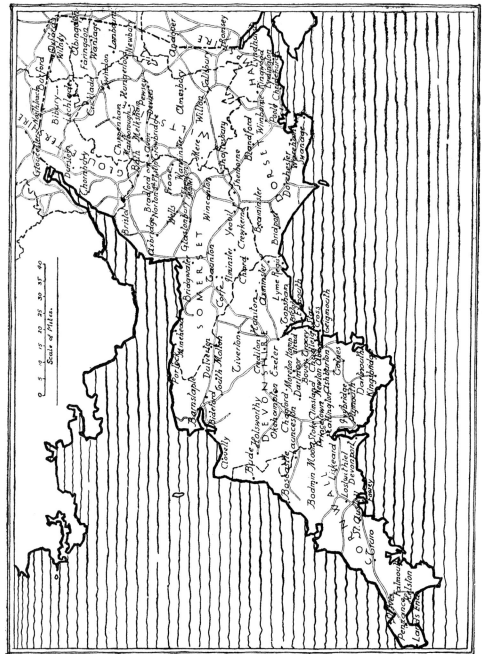

FIG. 262.—MAP OF SOUTH-WESTERN SECTION

FIG. 263. THE WHITE HART, DORCHESTER ON THAMES.

FIG. 264. THE KEIGWIN ARMS, MOUSEHOLE, CORNWALL.

FIG. 266.   THE KING'S ARMS, DORCHESTER. DORSET.
(*v. also Figs.* 118, 119.)

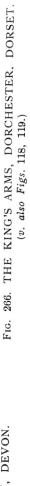

FIG. 265.   THE LION, ASHBURTON, DEVON.

Fig. 267.   THE SHIP, PORLOCK, SOMERSET.

FIG. 268. THE KING'S ARMS, OMBERSLEY, WORCESTERSHIRE.

FIG. 269. THE FALCON, CHESTER.

Blandford, threading a chain of pleasant places like Fontmell Magna, thence northwards to Sherborne or south-west to Dorchester ; the way offers many diversions to reach sequestered villages of typical Dorset thatch.   From Taunton, again, roads radiate in all directions ; the Combes of the Quantocks lie within easy reach ; north-west is the route to the Severn Sea and the charming group of little spots by Minehead and Porlock, such as Luscombe ; thence over the 1,300 feet of Exmoor to Lynton and the hills of North Devon.   An interesting feature of Somerset is the number of small market towns, such as Somerton, Glastonbury, Shepton Mallet, etc., many of which have the characteristic stone-built market houses.

In this west division will be seen an admixture of cob walling, thatch roofing, tiles, brick and stone, until walls of Cornish granite and Delabole slate are in sole use ; but at Penzance thatch is again to be seen.   The inns are most conspicuous along the main roads ; they range from the timber-built *George* at Salisbury to the brick inns at Exeter, the stone built King's Arms at Truro and the plain-fronted hostelries of Callington, Wadebridge and Bodmin.   There are the pictu-resque houses on the Bath Road, such as the King's Arms at Melksham, the Bear at Devizes, as well as the splendid mediæval inns at Glastonbury (Fig. 57) and Malmesbury, and a collection of inns can be named at Honiton, Axminster, Bridport, Wareham and Corfe (Fig. 87).   In Hampshire will be seen the long, low, two-storied inn roofed with thatch ; in Wiltshire the quasi-mediæval *George* at Amesbury (Fig. 55) and the Ship at Mere.   On Dartmoor there is the Warren House Inn, and at Princetown *The Plume of Feathers* (Fig. 126) ; Cornwall has the Bol Ventor on Bodmin Moor and *The Royal* at Falmouth, a spacious late Georgian house distinguished for its precise joinery and bold lettering.   This inn was once the rendezvous of passengers arriving by sailing packet from America.

The scenery in the south-west is an enlarged version, especially in Wilts and Somerset, of that in the south-east ; there are far-spreading distances viewed from the roads that traverse the ridges ; there is the interest of towns perched high like Shaftesbury, the wide panorama of undulating land across which fleecy clouds sweep above the Channel. The roads in their narrowness at times dip between high banks and hedges, for the most part long unaltered, excepting in surface.   From Amesbury they become a succession of lanes with awkward turns that sweep the traveller into such towns as Wincanton and Chard. With the exception of the Bath Road and the way from Andover, there

FIG. 270.—FORMERLY THE FIRST AND LAST INN, CROSCOMBE, SOMERSET

Sidney R. Jones, del.

is no sensation of being on a trunk road, the main thoroughfares having much in common with the winding by-lanes. It is surprising how the cross-roads from Bath and Bristol converge on minor towns and villages, forming an intricate network of roads which are rarely frequented by traffic, and these, as may be expected, have their quota of wayside halting places.

DIVISION III.—EASTERN

For the purposes of this touring guide it has been thought advisable to take a line from Ipswich to Cambridge and from thence to Buckden, on the Great North Road, the course of which is followed northward through Stamford and Newark ; then to Gainsborough and to the Humber for the western boundary of this section. The geology includes a certain amount of flint-bearing chalk, not very hilly, in Norfolk and Suffolk, the clay of the coast of Lincolnshire and the chalk and oolitic formation of the Lincolnshire Wolds. There is the red coral formation of the region near Cromer, and a vast area inland is occupied by the level of the alluvial Fens. In no wise can this area be termed industrial. There are the Cathedrals of Ely, Norwich, Lincoln, the ruined abbey of Croyland, the magnificent spires of Grantham and Heckington, the lantern at Boston and other historical buildings such as Tattershall Castle. The scenery has character ranging from the wooded slopes of Norfolk and Suffolk to the marshy plains near the Wash and along the coast to Grimsby, with the rolling wolds of Lincolnshire, the undulating lands of West Norfolk and the wide expanses of the Broads.

There is the maritime character of Yarmouth, King's Lynn and Boston, the Roman port near Wells, and reminiscences of intercourse in the Middle Ages with the Netherlands. We also recall the vanished industry of wool-stapling, the suggestion of Holland in the drainage, windmills that form a conspicuous part in the scenery, the long dykes and "20 foot cuts." The spires and towers of the churches stand up above the wind-swept flats, and the houses are for the most part unpretending as though fearful of the swampy ground from which they rise. Here the scenery is reversed, the skyscape is dominant and the land insignificant. The inns range from those of mid-Suffolk, which are of thatch and brick, or timber-built from a low wall, to such examples as the stone structure of *The Angel* at Grantham (Figs. 1, 13, 14). Brick is the chief material of East Anglia, with an occasional use of stone or flint chequered into squares or bonded with brick at the corners. The buildings

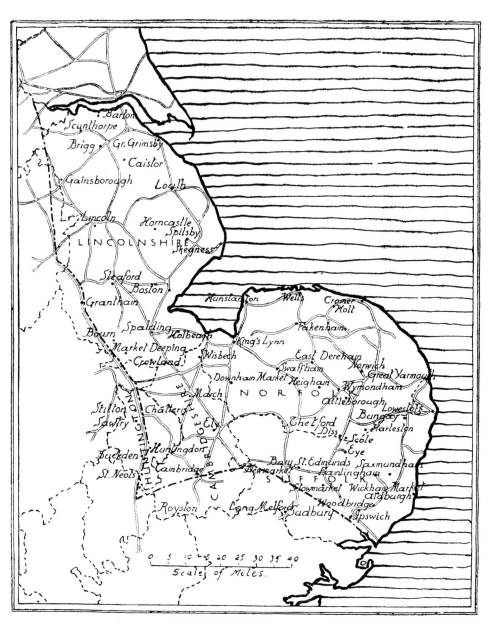

FIG. 271.—MAP OF EASTERN SECTION

have windows leaded, but on occasion heavily sashed, as exemplified in the streets of King's Lynn. The coast road from Yarmouth through Wells to Lynn, and then by Long Sutton to Spalding and Boston, is the main tourist route. The route from London runs direct to Norwich by Brandon Mills and Thetford, and is continued to Burnham Thorpe by Raynham. The way from Whitechapel Church goes to Lynn by Ely, and there is the road from Peterborough to Wisbech. To Lincoln there is the direct route from Peterborough through Bourne, with branches to Boston, and there are cross roads from Stamford to Bourne and Spalding, and others from Grantham to Sleaford, Horncastle and Spilsby, with branches to Lincoln, Beverley and Hull. In Lincolnshire will be encountered inns near the rivers, such as the Witham, and others near the canals. In Norfolk and Suffolk there are innumerable villages intact and unspoiled, for the depression which occurred in the wool-stapling industry gave impetus to agriculture, which, for a time, was revived, and here old customs and associations cling and village life is seen at its best. In Norwich the scene on market days is unforgettable. There are the carriers' carts from the neighbouring villages ; farmers and others come in to deal in cattle. There is excitement when the Assizes are on and the Eastern Circuit is in progress. Here are curious hilly streets where one expects from the map to find a city of the plains. Such towns as Wisbech, Spalding and Boston, as well as King's Lynn, have an interest, apart from the churches, which is explanatory of the wealth of other days. Wells is a town with one inn of repute and many smaller taverns near the quayside which are associated with the minor issues of coastal trade.

The exceptional scenic topography and history brings into prominence the charm of East Anglia. If all parts of England were alike, we should not have such a pleasant and varied picture, and the wonder is that so much is confined within the compass of a sea-girt island.

DIVISION IV.—THE MIDLANDS

By point of size alone the midland section is predominant, and here is the true centre of England. The division has for its western boundary the Welsh border, for its southern frontier a line from Gloucester to Oxford, thence north to Warwick and from there eastward to Bedford and Buckden. The Great North Road forms the eastern boundary, running from there to Newark and the Humber and thence to York,

FIG. 272.—MAP OF MIDLAND SECTION

and for the northern limit a line is taken through Knaresborough, Settle and Lancaster. There is but one coastal portion, extending from the south of Morecambe Bay to the Mersey. Five main roads radiating from London serve the Midlands; these have been touched upon in their southern beginnings. The geology over so large an area, as may be imagined, is diversified.

From the low clay lands of the Trent Valley, the limestone formation which fills so much of Derbyshire, the red sandstone of Nottingham, Stafford and the Birmingham district, while the great oolitic limestone formation of the Cotswolds crosses this district diagonally from Gloucester to near Stamford. There are also the isolated heights of the Malverns and the Wrekin. The older rocks bordering on Wales are limestone, with much of the slate and shale which belongs to the Silurian system, as may be seen exemplified in the tumbled country round Ludlow; much of Hereford, on the other hand, is of the old red sandstone.

In the richness of its landscapes, as of its historical and antiquarian objects, the midland division yields nothing to its neighbours. To the west there are hills which form the barriers to Wales, stretching from the Severn in the Valley of Evesham, through Worcester, and the river gaps to the Welsh coasts. Northward are the flatter, pastoral and well-timbered stretches of Cheshire, and then the flats of Lancashire rising centrally to bare limestone hills of the Peak. Much of the rest of the country is undulating grassland, and the Cotswolds have high, bare, rolling downs with stone walls, small wooded clumps and thickly villaged valleys. Birmingham and the Potteries, through intensive industrial development, represent a black furnace in the centre of umbrageous scenery, with contributory channels of blackness stretching northwards along artificial waterways.

This midland section makes one of the most delightful centres for touring. It is the very heart of England. It can be reached with little trouble from either of the diverging trunk roads, Ermine Street or Watling Street. Here will be encountered the stone tradition of the Cotswolds, varied with the black and white timbering of Worcestershire and the Welsh border counties, with castles at Coventry and Kenilworth, to the somewhat harsh brick of Whitchurch and Lichfield, as well as the rectitude of the buildings of Shrewsbury and Chester. Even in Lincolnshire, where brick predominates, stone is to be seen in juxtaposition. The Midlands owe part of their attractiveness to mediæval legend and action; the churches are rich and spacious, as at Coventry and Shrewsbury. There are the cathedral cities of Gloucester, Worcester,

FIG. 273.—THE SWAN, KNOWLE, WARWICKSHIRE.

W. H. Bidlake, del.

Fig. 274.   THE PHEASANT, BASSENTHWAITE, CUMBERLAND.

FIG. 275. THE GEORGE AND DRAGON, YARM ON TEES, YORKSHIRE.

FIG. 276. THE THREE NUNS, COOPER BRIDGE, YORKSHIRE.

Hereford, Chester, Lichfield, as well as picturesque castles. There are the hill towns of the Peak District and the picturesque river valleys of Yorkshire. Nearer London is the cathedral city of Oxford, and such interesting towns as Leamington, Towcester, Banbury, Atherstone, Stoke and Whitchurch. There are minor towns, such as Daventry, Dunchurch, Chipping Campden, Leominster and Ledbury. After traversing the high, bare, rolling limestone downs of the Cotswolds, with their characteristic stone buildings roofed with stone slates, the Vale of Evesham forms an idyllic rambling district, in which the villages, with their inns, are unsurpassed for character and charm. The course of the Avon is studded with the spots mentioned by Shakespeare, all happy in appearance, and many of the stone-built villages dotted at the foot of the Cotswold escarpment, from Campden to Cheltenham, contrast agreeably with the half-timber and thatch of such hamlets as the Combertons, Castle Elmley, Cropthorne and many another. Any of these, of either of the two types, would take high rank in the interesting but futile competition for the most picturesque place in England. Here are long stretches of roads, some running for 30 miles without touching a town, such as the Old Watling Street from the entrance to Weedon, to Atherstone, and again where it skirts Lichfield and traverses unspoiled country by the inn of the Three Crosses in the direction of Shrewsbury. There are roads originating from Worcester city striking into the very heart of the Midlands through leafy lanes and villages of arcadian solitude. The landscape is not dramatic, except near the Welsh border ; it is mainly a succession of woods and commons, but the abruptness of the change when the centres of industry are reached is most marked. It is advisable to arrange tours to avoid such places as Birmingham, although the centre of the latter city has much to interest and the place as a travelling centre is unrivalled. It must not be forgotten that for many centuries the recognised route from London to Scotland was through the midland region by the way of St. Albans, Chester, Lancaster and so to Carlisle.

There are a few stone-built inns in the Midlands which have preserved their original features intact. *The Lygon Arms* at Broadway (Figs. 85, 95) is well known, but many additions have been made to the original house, with due observance of local character. The best timbered inns are to be seen at Shrewsbury, Ludlow and Chester, with a sprinkling in places adjacent to these centres. There is the curious patchwork house at Banbury, the stone-built *Saracen's Head*, now *The Pomfret Arms*, at Towcester (Fig. 86), and that magnificent specimen of masonry representing the Cotswold tradition, the Haycock at Wansford (Figs. 20-22). Stamford can boast some good inns apart from the prominent Stamford Hotel (Figs. 103, 104, 116). They are of Cotswold extraction, with bay windows and leaded lights, a distinctive feature being the prevalence of the small gable and its adjustment to the bay window by means of two kneelers.

An entertaining and original method of touring is to follow to their sources the course of some of the less known rivers, such as the Cotswold Evenlode and Windrush, or, in the west midland country, the Teme, from its confluence with the Severn at Worcester right into the Welsh hills, the Lugg throughout West Herefordshire, the Frome, the Monnow and the Usk in Monmouthshire. Occasionally a well-made road threads the banks, but often marsh and flood have precluded the making of a level track, and the traveller wanders up and down through little hamlets by a circuitous route. But in any case the gain would be great in access to out-of-the-way spots and to a great diversity of landscape. Only the Wye has thus habitually been explored, and then the once fashionable " Wye tour " often omitted the most attractive portion—above Hereford westward to the Welsh border at Hay.

SECTION V.—NORTH

This comprises the four northern counties and the portions of Lancashire and Yorkshire included in the line from Lancaster through Settle to York and Beverley and thence to the Humber. There are few tourists who bestow much time to the northern counties, except to make special pilgrimages to the Lake District or the moors. There are the invalids who frequent Buxton and Harrogate, and others, more robust, explore the central Pennine Range ; but motorists, with Scotland before them, are apt to neglect the northern counties as they hurry through.

This section is largely highland, and many of the older geological formations are represented. On the east is the Plain of York, bounded on the north by the low, rolling Cleveland hills with their ironstone, the central limestone backbone of the Pennines, extending both east and west. Much of West Yorkshire is moorland. Durham is largely moorland hills, with extensive colleries, and there is a large colliery plain north of Newcastle, though Western Northumberland has big rolling hills up to the Cheviots. On the west side the Lancashire country round the coast is flat, and then, proceeding north, the traveller

FIG. 277.—MAP OF NORTHERN SECTION

encounters the Shap Fells with the abrupt shales and slates of the Lake District hills, which give way to the flat plain north of Carlisle.

Amongst southerners there has always existed a feeling of apprehension regarding the distant north, which may have survived from Roman times when the country beyond the wolds of York was almost entirely abandoned. Even in the Middle Ages travellers between London and Scotland kept to the main roads ; they feared the hillmen from the Pennines as well as the lawless Borderers. Racial distinctions between north and south have long been sharply defined, hence it is we have a section of England with its own customs rather aloof from the urbanity of the south. This is not to say that Yorkshire, Lancashire, Northumberland, Westmorland, Cumberland and Durham are devoted individually and collectively to a similar interest to that which enriches the southern shires. Local materials and harder methods of living in the past produced a system of building which is as markedly original as that of Cornwall. It was Ruskin who praised the cottage homes of Westmorland, and it remains for others to describe and study the dignified plain stone buildings. The chief inns will be found, as might be expected, on the main roads. There is the house at Greta Bridge described by Dickens (Fig. 226) ; there are the inns of Durham, and the stone built *Turk's Head* in Newcastle (Fig. 219). The Lakeside inns of Westmorland and Cumberland (Fig. 274), the posthouses of Alnwick and Berwick, as well as the chain of diminutive taverns which stand on either side of the road between Lancaster and Carlisle, whose antiquity could speak of " great doings " as well as of the incidents of hasty journeys to Gretna. Northern inns when Johnson and Boswell were on the road were not renowned for comfort ; it was sufficient to obtain a seat at the fireside and a rough bed. The case is different with the inns of York. There the mediæval inns, long since transformed into tenements and business premises, have gone into retirement. York, unlike London, can still show inns with entrances for waggons and coaches, thus having an affinity with Chester ; at one time these cities were the twin hubs of wheeled traffic to the north. The northern region is bound up with mediæval history and has a long story of wars and rebellion. It has always been the most political of all England, from the Wars of the Roses to the Jacobite Rising. As is to be expected the inn of antique pretension is only to be found in the old towns served by the east and west coast routes. Between these points there was little development, but the 19th century brought industry into the intervening spaces, obliterating many local features.

And so this chapter of suggested methods of working out tours is brought to a close. The inns in all parts of the country open up a fresh page of general history, showing the intimate life of the past and present which has ebbed and flowed and left its mark. It was not until late in the seventeenth century that inns began to be noted by writers. In the coaching days travellers were more critical and inn-keepers did their best to please by providing good furniture and table appointments. We know from Goldsmith's description how travellers were apt to mistake an antique mansion for an inn (Fig. 182), and it is pleasant to think that the best of English inns as they stand to-day have much of the grace of the country house.

We take leave of the inns, the roads and the associations of travel with mixed feelings, conscious of the omission of much that should have been included in the story. We find ourselves in the position of knowing the chief facts of the subject, but aware that many will look in vain for some particular inn of their own selection. We are full of solicitude for the disappointment of others, but have for excuse the enormous mass of material that almost defies presentation, apart from any possibility of record other than in an encyclopædia. To us and to others there is the charm of something yet to be accomplished, of many inns to be enjoyed and fresh incidents to be imagined. The inns of England are the very best of their kind, so is it not significant that they are regarded with veneration?

APPENDIX

TOPOGRAPHICAL LIST OF OLD INNS

I.—South-Eastern Section

BEDFORDSHIRE :
Ampthill : Rising Sun
    Crown and Sceptre
    King's Arms
    King's Head
    White Hart
Barford (Gt.) : Swan
Bedford : George
    Red Lion
    Swan
    Bridge
Biggleswade : Swan
Clophill : Compasses
    Flying Horse
Dunstable : Red Lion
    Saracen's Head
    Sugar Loaf
Eaton Socon : White Horse
Elstow : Swan
Hockcliffe : White Horse
Leighton Buzzard : Swan
Luton : George
    Red Lion
Maulden : White Hart
Tempsford : Anchor
Turvey : Five Fishes
Woburn : Bedford Arms

BERKSHIRE :
Abingdon : Lion
Hartford Bridge :
    White Lion
Hurley : Bell
Maidenhead : Bear
Newbury : Chequers
    Jack o' Newbury
    Pelican
Pangbourn : George
Reading : Ship
Shillingford : Shillingford
    Hotel
Thatcham : King's Head
    White Hart
Theale : Old Angel
Wallingford : George
    Lamb
Waltham St. Lawrence : Bell
Windsor : Star and Garter
    White Hart

BERKSHIRE—*Con.*
Wokingham : Rose
Woolhampton : Angel

BUCKINGHAMSHIRE :
Amersham : Crown
    Griffin
Aylesbury : Bell
    George
    King's Head
Beaconsfield :
    Royal Saracen's
    Royal White Hart
Bierton : Red Lion
Buckingham : Swan and
    Castle
    White Hart
Chalfont St. Peter :
    Greyhound
Chesham : Crown
    George
Colnbrook : Ostrich
Denham : Swan
High Wycombe : Falcon
    Red Lion
Marlow : Chequers
    Compleat Angler
    Crown
Newport Pagnell : Anchor
    Swan
Olney : Bull
Princes Risborough :
    George and Dragon
Slough : Old Crown
    Royal
Stokenchurch : King's Arms
Stony Stratford : Bull
    Cock
Stratford, Fenny : Bull
    Cock
    Swan
Wendover : Nag's Head
    Packhorse
    Red Lion
Whitchurch : White Hart

ESSEX :
Braintree : Horns
    White Hart

ESSEX—*Con.*
Chelmsford : Lion and
    Lamb
    White Hart
Chigwell : King's Head
    (Maypole)
Colchester : Cups
    George
    Red Lion
    Three
    Horseshoes
Dunmow : Saracen's Head
Harwich : White Hart
Maldon : Blue Boar
    King's Head
Ongar : King's Head
Paglesham : Plough and
    Sail
Southend : Royal Hotel
Saffron Walden : Rose and
    Crown
Thaxted : Swan
Waltham : White Hart
Waltham Cross :
    Four Swans
Witham : White Hart
    Spread Eagle

HAMPSHIRE (EAST) :
Alresford : Swan
Alton : Swan
Basingstoke : Red Lion
Bishop's Waltham : Crown
Fareham : Red Lion
Hartley Row : Lamb
Hinton Admiral : Cat and
    Fiddle
Hurstbourne Tarrant :
    George
Liphook : Angel
Odiham : George
    Tuns
Petersfield : Red Lion
Portsmouth : George
Southampton : Dolphin
Twyford : King's Arms
Winchester : George
    Hostel of God
    Begot

HERTFORDSHIRE :
Baldock : Rose and Crown
Barley : Fox and Hounds
Barnet : Duke of York
    Hart's Horns
    Red Lion
Berkhampstead :
    King's Arms
    Swan
Bishops Stortford : Chequers
    George
    White
      Horse
Buntingford : George and
    Dragon
Digswell Hill : Waggon and
    Horses
Hatfield : Eight Bells
    Red Lion
    Salisbury Arms
Hertford : Blue Boy
    Dimsdale Arms
    Green Dragon
Hitchin : Cock
    Cooper's Arms
    Sun
    Three Tuns
Hoddesdon : Bull
Redbourn : Bull
Royston : Bull
    Crown
St. Albans : Fighting Cocks
    George
    Peahen
    Red Lion
    White Hart
St. Michaels, St. Albans :
    Black Lion
Tring : Bell
    Rose and Crown
Ware : Saracen's Head
Water End : Red Lion
Watford : Clarendon
    Essex Arms
    George
    Rose and Crown

KENT :
Bromley : Royal Bell
Canterbury : Falstaff
    Flying Horse
    Fountain
    Rose
Cranbrook : George
    Chequers
Dartford : Bull
Dover : Ship
Farnborough : Tumble
    Down Dick
Faversham : Ship

KENT—*Con.*
Great Mongeham :
    Three Horseshoes
Otford : Bull
Rochester : Bull and
    Victoria
    George
    Bull
Sandwich : Bell
Sevenoaks : Royal Oak
    Royal Crown
    White Hart
Sittingbourne : Bull
    Red Lion
Tenterden : White Lion
Tonbridge : Angel
    Chequers
    Rose and Crown
Tunbridge Wells : Castle
Westerham : George and
    Dragon
    King's Arms
Wingham : Lion

LONDON :
Fleet Street : Cheshire
    Cheese
Greenwich : Ship
Hampstead : Bull and Bush
    Flask
    Jack Straw's
    Castle
Limehouse : Grapes
Southwark : George

MIDDLESEX :
Edgware : Chandos Arms
Highgate : Flask
Southall : Whitehall
Uxbridge : Crown and
    Treaty

OXFORDSHIRE :
Bicester : Crown
Benson : Crown
Clifton Hampden : Barley
    Mow
Dorchester : George
    Golden Cross
Goring and Streatley :
    Miller of Mansfield
    Swan
Henley : Angel
    Bull
    Catherine Wheel
    Little White Hart
    Red Lion
Oxford : Mitre
Tetsworth : Swan

OXFORDSHIRE—*Con.*
Thame : Hog's Head
    Spread Eagle

SURREY :
Blechingly : Stag
    White Hart
Chertsey : Crown
Chiddingfold : Crown
Cobham : White Lion
Croydon : Greyhound
Dorking : Red Lion
    Star and Garter
    White Horse
Epsom : King's Head
Esher : Bear
Farnham : Bush
Godalming : Angel
    King's Arms
Guildford : Angel
    Lion
Hook : White Hart
Kingston : Sun
Kingston Vale : Plough
Leatherhead : Swan
Ockley : Red Lion
Oxted : Bell
Reigate : Swan
    White Hart
Ripley : Talbot
Shere : White Horse
Sutton : Cock

SUSSEX :
Alfriston : Star
Battle : George
    (Pilgrim's Hostel)
Brighton : Bedford
    Old Ship
Chichester : Anchor and
    Dolphin
Cuckfield : King's Head
East Grinstead : Dorset
    Arms
Fittleworth : Swan
Hailsham : George
Horsham : Anchor
    Black Horse
    King's Head
Lewes : Crown
    White Hart
Midhurst : Angel
    Spread Eagle
Petworth : Swan
Robertsbridge : Seven Stars
Rye : Mermaid
Sedlescombe : Queen's
    Head
Uckfield : Maiden's Head

II.—South-Western Section

BERKSHIRE (West) :
Faringdon : Bell
      Crown
Lambourn : Red Lion
Wantage : Bear

CORNWALL :
Bodmin Moor : Bol Ventor
Boscastle : Wellington
Bude : Falcon
Callington : Golding's Hotel
Falmouth : Royal
Fowey : Lugger
Helston : Angel
Lands End : First and Last
      House
Launceston : Castle
      King's Arms
      White Hart
Liskeard : Stag
      Webb's
Lostwithiel : Royal Talbot
Penzance : Star
St. Austell : Queen's Head
St. Ives : Golden Lion
      Tregenna Castle
Stoke Climsland :
      Half Moon
Truro : King's Arms
      Red Lion
      Royal

DEVONSHIRE :
Ashburton : Golden Lion
Axminster : George
Barnstaple : Royal
Bideford : Royal
Bicton : King's Arms
Bovey Tracey : Dolphin
Chagford : Three Crowns
Chudleigh : Clifford Arms
Clovelly : New Inn
Crediton : Ship
Dartmoor : Warren House
      Inn
Dartmouth : Royal Castle
Devonport : Royal Hotel
Dulverton : Lamb
      Red Lion
Exeter : Clarendon
      London
Exmouth : London
      Royal Beacon
      Thorn
Holsworthy : White Hart

DEVONSHIRE—*Con.*
Honiton :   Dolphin
      (Banfield's)
Ivybridge : London
Kingsbridge : King's Arms
Moreton Hampstead :
      White Hart
Newton Abbot : Globe
Okehampton : White Hart
Plymouth : Royal
Princetown : Duchy
      Plume of
      Feathers
Star Cross : Courtenay Arms
South Molton : George
      Unicorn
Tavistock : Bedford
Teignmouth : Royal
Tiverton : Angel
Topsham : Salutation
Totnes : Royal Seven Stars

DORSET :
Beaminster : White Hart
Blandford : Crown
Bridport : Bull
      Greyhound
Dorchester : Antelope
      King's Arms
      White Hart
Lyme Regis : Royal Lion
      Three Cups
Poole : Antelope
      King Charles
      London
Shaftesbury : Grosvenor
Sherborne : Digby
Swanage : Ship
Wareham : Black Bear
Wimborne : Coach and
      Horses
      Crown
      King's Head

GLOUCESTERSHIRE
  (South) :
Bibury : Swan
Bristol : Royal Western
      Hotel
Lechlade : New Inn
Northleach : Wheatsheaf

HAMPSHIRE (West) :
Andover : Star and Garter
      White Hart
Christchurch : King's Arms

GLOUCESTERSHIRE—*Con.*
Lymington : Angel
      Old Toll House
Lyndhurst : Crown
      Stag
Ringwood : Crown
      White Hart
Romsey : White Horse

OXFORDSHIRE (West) :
Burford : Bull
Witney : Marlborough Arms

SOMERSET :
Axbridge : George
Bath : Angel
      York House
Bridgwater : White Hart
Chard : George
Corfe : Greyhound
Crewkerne : George
Dunster : Luttrell Arms
Frome : Crown
      George
Glastonbury : Crown
      George (Pil-
      grims' Inn)
Ilminster : George
Minehead : Plume of
      Feathers
      Wellington
Norton St. Philip : George
Porlock : Ship
Shepton Mallet : Hare and
      Hounds
Taunton : Castle
Wells : Mitre
      Red Lion
      Star
      Swan
Wincanton : Bear
      Greyhound
Yeovil : Mermaid
      Pen Mill
      Three Choughs

WILTSHIRE :
Amesbury : George
Bradford-on-Avon : Swan
Chippenham : Angel
Cricklade : White Hart
Devizes : Bear
Hungerford : Black Bear
      Three Swans

WILTSHIRE—*Con.*
Marlborough : Castle and
Ball
Five Alls
Melksham : King's Arms
Mere : Ship

WILTSHIRE—*Con.*
Pewsey : Greyhound
Salisbury : Crown
George
Red Lion
White Hart

WILTSHIRE—*Con.*
Swindon : Goddard Arms
King's Arms
Trowbridge : George
Warminster : Bath Arms
Wilton : Pembroke Arms

III.—Eastern Section

CAMBRIDGESHIRE :
Cambridge : Blue Boar
Bull
Red Lion
Chatteris : Old George
Ely : Bell
Lamb
March : Old Griffin
Royston : Bull
Wisbech : Rose and Crown
Ship

HUNTINGDONSHIRE :
Buckden : Falcon
George
Lion
Huntingdon : Bridge
George
St. Neots : Cross Keys
Sawtry : Globe
Stilton : Bell

LINCOLNSHIRE :
Barton : George
Boston : Red Lion
White Hart
Bourn : Angel
Bull
Brigg : Angel
Caistor : Red Lion
Crowland : George
Gainsborough : White Hart
Grantham : Angel
Royal
Beehive
George
Great Grimsby : Ship
Holbeach : Chequers

LINCOLNSHIRE—*Con.*
Horncastle : Bull
Red Lion
Lincoln : Saracen's Head
Spread Eagle
White Hart
Louth : King's Head
Market Deeping : New Inn
Scunthorpe : Blue Bell
Skegness : Lion
Sleaford : Bristol Arms
White Hart
Spalding : Red Lion
White Hart
Spilsby : George
White Hart
Stamford : George
Stamford Hotel

NORFOLK :
Attleborough : Angel
Griffin
Cromer : Old Red Lion
Diss : Crown
Downham Market : Castle
Crown
East Dereham : King's
Arms
Fakenham : Crown
Lion
Great Yarmouth : Angel
Harleston : Swan
Heigham : Dolphin
Holt : Feathers
Hunstanton : Globe
Golden Lion
King's Lynn : Duke's Head
Globe

NORFOLK—*Con.*
Lowestoft : Crown
Royal
Norwich : Bell
Castle
Maid's Head
Scole : White Hart
Swaffham : George
Thetford : Anchor
Bell
Watton : Crown
Wells : Crown
Wymondham : King's Head

SUFFOLK :
Aldburgh : Railway
Bungay : King's Head
Bury St. Edmunds : Angel
Half Moon
Eye : White Lion
Framlingham : Crown
Ipswich : Crown and Anchor
Great White Horse
Half Moon
Long Melford : Castle
Newmarket : Crown
Rutland Arms
White Hart
Saxmundham : Bell
White Hart
Stanton : Rose and Crown
Stowmarket : Fox
King's Head
Sudbury : Rose and Crown
Wickham Market :
White Hart
Woodbridge : Bell
Crown

IV.—Midland Section

CHESHIRE :
Alderley Edge : De Trafford
Arms
Altrincham : Unicorn
Cheadle : George and Dragon
White Hart
Chester : Bear and Billet
Falcon
Feathers

CHESHIRE—*Con.*
Congleton : Bull's Head
Lion and Swan
Crewe : Crewe Arms
Knutsford : Angel
Royal George
Macclesfield : Macclesfield
Arms

CHESHIRE—*Con.*
Nantwich : Crown
Lamb
Plumbley : Smoker
Sandbach : Bear
Tabley : Windmill
Tarporley : Alvanley Arms
Swan

DERBYSHIRE:
Ashbourne: Green Man
Bakewell: Rutland Arms
Buxton: George
       Shakespeare
       Old Hall
Chapel-en-le-Frith:
       King's Arms
Derby: Midland
Dovedale: Black Man's
       Head
       Green Man
Glossop: Norfolk Arms
Ilkeston: Rutland
Matlock: Crown
Rowsley: Peacock

GLOUCESTERSHIRE
(North):
Bourton-on-the-Water:
       New Inn
Cheltenham: Fleece
       Plough
       Queen's
       Royal
Chipping Campden:
       Lygon Arms
       Noel Arms
Dursley: Bell
       Castle
Gloucester: New Inn
Moreton in Marsh:
       Redesdale Arms
       Royal
       White Hart
Stow on the Wold: Talbot
       Unicorn
Tewkesbury: Bell
       Berkeley
       Arms
       Hop Pole
       Sun
       Swan
       Wheatsheaf
Winchcombe: George
Thornbury: Swan

HEREFORDSHIRE:
Bromyard: Falcon
       Hop Pole
Hereford: Green Dragon
       Mitre
Ledbury: Feathers
       Royal Oak
Leominster: Royal Oak
       Talbot
Ross: King's Head
       Man of Ross
       Swan

LANCASHIRE:
Accrington: Hargreave
       Arms
Blackburn: White Bull
       Old Bull
Burnley: Bull
       Old Sparrow Hawk
       Thorn
Garstang: Royal Oak
Lancaster: County
       King's Arms
Lytham: Clifton Arms
Preston: Bull and Royal
Sale: Brooklands
Todmorden: White Hart

LEICESTERSHIRE:
Ashby-de-la-Zouch: Royal
Hinckley: George
Leicester: Bell
       George
       Stag & Pheasant
       Wyvern
Loughborough:
       King's Head
       Old Bull's Head
Lutterworth:
       Denbigh Arms
       Hind
Market Harborough:
       Angel
       Peacock
       Swan
       Three Swans
Melton Mowbray: George

NORTHAMPTONSHIRE:
Aynho: Cartwright Arms
Brackley: Crown
Daventry: Saracen's Head
       Wheatsheaf
Deene: Sea Horse
Gretton: White Hart
Kettering: George
       Royal
Northampton: Angel
       Cock
       Peacock
       Plough
       Ram
Oundle: Talbot
       White Lion
Peterborough: Angel
Towcester: Pomfret Arms
       Talbot
       Folly
Wansford: Haycock
Weldon Magna: King's
       Arms
Wellingborough: Angel
       Hind

NOTTINGHAMSHIRE:
East Retford: White Hart
Newark: Clinton Arms
       Ram
       White Horse
Nottingham: Black Boy
       Flying Horse
       George
Ollerton: Hop Pole
Southwell: Saracen's Head
Tuxford: Newcastle Arms
Worksop: Lion
       Royal

OXFORDSHIRE (North):
Banbury: Red Lion
       Reindeer
       White Lion
Chipping Norton:
       Crown and Anchor
       White Hart
Deddington: Unicorn
Woodstock: Bear

RUTLANDSHIRE:
Oakham: Crown
       George
Uppingham: Crown
       Falcon

SHROPSHIRE:
Bridgnorth: Crown
       Falcon
Church Stretton:
       Longsword
Ellesmere: Black Lion
Ludlow: Angel
       Bull
       Feathers
Market Drayton:
       Corbet Arms
Much Wenlock:
       Gaskell Arms
Newport: Barley Mow
Oswestry: Wynnstay
Shrewsbury: Crown
       Raven
Wellington: Charlton Arms
       Wrekin
Wem: Castle
       White Horse
Whitchurch: Swan

STAFFORDSHIRE:
Brereton: Bear's Head
Burton-upon-Trent:
       White Hart
Eccleshall: Crown
       King's Arms
Leek: George
       Red Lion

STAFFORDSHIRE—*Con.*
Lichfield : Four Crosses
George
King's Head
Swan
Longton : Crown & Anchor
Newcastle-under-Lyme :
Borough Arms
Penkridge : Littleton Arms
White Hart
Rugeley : Shrewsbury Arms
Stafford : Swan
Vine
Tamworth : Castle
Peel Arms
Uttoxeter : White Hart

WARWICKSHIRE :
Alcester : Globe
Atherstone : Red Lion
Coventry : King's Head
Kenilworth :
King's Arms and Castle
Queen and Castle
Leamington : Crown
Leamington Spa : Regent

WARWICKSHIRE—*Con.*
Nuneaton : Gull
Rugby : Royal George
Three Horseshoes
Southam : Craven Arms
Stratford-on-Avon :
Falcon
Red House and
Golden
Shakespeare
Swan's Nest
Warwick : Crown
Warwick Arms
Woolpack

WORCESTERSHIRE :
Bewdley : George
Broadway : Fish
Lygon Arms
Bromsgrove : Golden Cross
Chaddesley Corbet : Talbot
Droitwich : Swan
Evesham : Crown
Great Malvern : Beauchamp
Kidderminster : Lion

WORCESTERSHIRE—*Con.*
Ombersley : Half-Way House
King's Arms
Pershore : Royal Three Tuns
Redditch : Unicorn
Stourport : Swan
Tenbury : Swan
Upton-on-Severn :
White Hart
White Lion
Worcester : Crown
Star

YORKSHIRE :
Doncaster : Reindeer
Harrogate : George
Leeds : Boar's Head
Golden Lion
Griffin
Pontefract : Red Lion
Rotherham : Crown
Sheffield : King's Head
Skipton : Black Horse
Ship
Wakefield : Strafford Arms
White Horse

V.—Northern Section

CUMBERLAND :
Brampton : White Lion
Carlisle : Crown and Mitre
Red Lion
Cockermouth : Glebe
Egremont : King's Arms
Keswick : Old George
Pheasant
Maryport : Golden Lion
Penrith : Crown
Wigton : Kildare

DURHAM :
Barnard Castle :
King's Head
Darlington : King's Head
Durham : Three Tuns
Rose and Crown

LANCASHIRE (North) :
Clitheroe : Swan and Royal
Coniston : Waterhead
Sun
Ulverston : Sun

NORTHUMBERLAND :
Alnwick : White Swan
Star
Plough
Belford : Blue Bell
Berwick-on-Tweed :
King's Arms

NORTHUMBERLAND—*Con,*
Blanchland : Crewe Arms
Hexham : Royal
Abbey

WESTMORLAND :
Appleby : King's Head
Tufton Arms
Brough : George
Castle
Grasmere : Swan
Red Lion
Kendal : King's Arms
Kirby Lonsdale : Royal
Kirkby Stephen :
King's Arms
Black Bull
Middleton-in-Teesdale :
Cleveland Arms

YORKSHIRE :
Barnby Moor : The Bell
Bawtry : The Crown
Bedale : Black Swan
Beverley : Beverley Arms
Boroughbridge :
Three Greyhounds
Great Driffield : Bell
Buck
Guisborough : Ward Arms
Helmsley : Black Swan
Faversham Arms

YORKSHIRE—*Con.*
Hull : The George
Ilkley : Crescent
Leyburn : Golden Lion
Market Weighton :
Londesborough
Northallerton : Golden Lion
Otley : Royal White Horse
Black Horse
Pickering : Black Swan
White Swan
Pocklington : Feathers
Richmond : King's Head
Ripon : Unicorn
Sedbergh : White Hart
Bull
Selby : The George
Settle : Golden Lion
Tadcaster : Londesborough
Thirsk : Fleece
Three Tuns
Thorne : White Hart
Whitby : Angel
Witherby : Brunswick
Angel
Yarm-on-Tees : George and
Dragon
York : White Swan
Black Swan
Windmill
Harker's

INDEX

NOTE.—*Figures which appear in heavier type denote those pages on which illustrations are to be found.*